POWERFUL
CATHOLIC
MASCULINITY

POWERFUL CATHOLIC MASCULINITY

BY MICHAEL JAQUITH

EVER **CATHOLIC**

SANDPOINT, IDAHO

Ever Catholic
Copyright © by Michael Jaquith. All rights reserved.

Book Design and Illustrations by Kylie Spizale.
Copyright © All rights reserved.

ISBN: 978-1-946076-12-0

Published by Ever Catholic, Sandpoint, Idaho

First Edition: November 2025

For information about special discounts for bulk purchases,
please contact Michael Jaquith at
michael@catholiclifecoachformen.com

INTRODUCTION

Most people skip introductions. I will be brief.

This book can change your life. Its ideas will challenge what you think it means to be manly.

This book is based upon hundreds of self-help books, thousands of hours coaching others, and the wisdom collected by all the men who have poured into my life.

The ideas in this book will not be easy, comfortable, or popular. They will challenge you to think very differently. They require time and effort, but as with weightlifting, keep doing the reps, and you will become stronger.

I challenge you to put on your armor, gird your loins, and commit to the combat.

CHAPTER ONE
POLARIZATION

Imagine the scene:

Across the reception hall, a young woman's eyes land upon a good-looking man. Her eyes sparkle and linger on him a moment longer than necessary. As he notices her attention, a small smile tugs the edges of his lips up. He returns her gaze, giving thanks that God gave him such a great woman to be his wife. It's been forty years since they were last in this hall, but with effort, the attraction is still powerful.

Attraction makes us feel alive, energized, and complete. Attraction changes an ordinary interaction into some-thing explosive and memorable. But how does it work?

Many factors contribute to attraction, including age, interests, appearance, and values. These can be complex and changing. However, there is one factor that is universally part of the attraction and is much simpler. I call it "polarization."

I'm a chemist by training, so I will define polarization by starting with a chemistry metaphor. Consider electrons and protons; they have opposite charges and an extremely high attraction. Imagine if you and I were together when suddenly you had 1% more electrons while I had 1% more protons. The attractive force created would be strong enough to move the earth itself! The concept of "opposites attract" is found across the universe—including our human biology.

Instead of positive and negative, the human polarization is "masculine" and "feminine." These are descriptions of ways to see and interact with the world. Don't confuse "masculine" and "feminine" with "male" and "female." Men and women can each be either masculine or feminine at different times. Both sexes tend to operate out of a more masculine perspective in the workplace. Both tend to operate more in a more feminine way when caring for children. When a man leans into his masculinity and a woman into her femininity, the attraction is maximized. You see this polarization even within same-sex relationships: There is always one more masculine partner and one who is more feminine.

I'll explore polarization further from a chemistry perspective. Water is a funny molecule. It's a tiny and light molecule—by all standard rules, it should be a gas. Yet, the polarization between the oxygen and hydrogen atoms changes everything. Instead of a free-flowing gas at room temperature, you have strong connective bonds that hold the water molecules together as a liquid. Polarization doesn't only create attraction—it builds bonds. Bonds hold us together.

Sometimes, married couples lose their polarity. Suppose the man ceases to be masculine and the woman ceases to be feminine. In that case, the attraction is lost, and the bond holding them together diminishes. Unless another, deeper bond exists, the partners go their separate ways. There are numerous examples of this today.

Polarization, even in chemistry, is complex. Highly polarized molecules can increase the polarization of other nearby molecules. For example, in a battery, each electrode creates a layer of oppositely polarized molecules. The same is true in relationships. If a husband leans into his masculinity, his wife will likely start to polarize as well, though perhaps slowly.

When a husband becomes more masculine, his wife will often become more feminine in response. Similarly, a highly feminized woman will usually draw out masculinity in the men she is around. Sadly, spouses frequently try to change their partners when changing themselves would have a far more significant impact!

Of course, biological attraction is much more complicated than electric attraction. I'll introduce many models in this book to help readers understand it. Please remember—all models are wrong. Any model is, by definition, not entirely accurate. The good ones, however, are helpful. Allow me to explain by example.

The other day, I was driving down the road with a few kids in the car. At a red light, I turned right after a brief (and perhaps incomplete) stop. My justice-loving kiddo quickly pointed out that I had run the red light and had made a mistake. She further added that I had been "speeding" by going five miles per hour over the limit. I explained that traffic laws are a "model" for how we're supposed to drive. They are helpful, for sure, but no one really follows all of them. This principle is also applicable in the legal system, in our food production, and wherever humans are involved.

Human attraction and relationships are far more complex than traffic rules. I'll use several models to help explain different facets. None of them is a perfect fit, but hopefully, each model will help further build upon the previous.

Many people today, raised in twisted modern ideology, do not even understand what a male and female are. When Matt Walsh created a comical documentary attempting to answer the question of "what is a woman," it quickly became apparent that modern ideology is confused. During his interviews with tribal people, however, even the question seemed absurd to them. Of course, they know what a woman is! The innate knowledge of the sexes and how they interact has been preserved in communal memories for countless generations—only recently have we thrown it out. Our current definitions are so far off that we need to start again. These models will help you see these dynamics differently.

The first model for human attraction within romantic relationships is that of polarization. If you want your wife to be more attracted to you, lean into your masculinity. Not only will that directly increase her attraction to you, but it will likely encourage her to lean into her femininity. This polarization increases mutual attraction! Be masculine—unreservedly and unapologetically. Do not, however, be a jerk to your wife.

CHAPTER TWO
ROCKS AND WAVES

Imagine the following fight between a husband and wife. You can adapt it to one of your fights if it happens to fit:

Emily texts Ted at work, "I can't wait for this party tonight; I'm so excited to go with you!"

Right before leaving, Ted's boss asked for one more thing. After finishing, Ted arrievs home twenty minutes later than he had told Emily he would arrive. Unfortunately, she does not take it well.

"Where have you been? We were supposed to leave ten minutes ago, but now we'll be late! Don't you care for me at all?"

Surprised, Ted attempts to calm her down: "Don't overreact! I'm sure we'll be fine. It's okay if we walk in a few minutes late. The party doesn't really matter anyway! You don't need to be so worked up."

"I don't even want to go at all now! I can't stand you; all you do is make my life miserable. You don't care about me and are just so thoughtless! You've ruined everything! You know I hate to be late!"

Ted has a hard day at work and doesn't have the energy to deal with this. "Fine, I never wanted to go anyway! If you had planned it better, this wouldn't have happened. I just wish you weren't so prideful and vain. You don't have to ruin the whole night by being ten minutes late!"

If you're married, you know that whatever happens next will not likely draw Ted and Emily closer together. What did Ted do wrong in this story? Perhaps he could have been more timely or planned better, but I claim there were other opportunities for him to recover the night. Ted failed to be masculine and failed to leave space for Emily's femininity. After explaining the Rocks and Waves model, we'll return to this unfortunate conversation.

Have you ever been to the Pacific Northwest coastline? I lived in Portland for several years, and my wife and I regularly headed to the Oregon coast. Imagine large ocean waves rolling towards the shore, smashing gloriously against jagged rock formations. The spray and splash would travel through the air, delighting watchers. It is a dance between the ocean and the beach.

Please consider this image as the basis for the next model I propose. Again, models are entirely accurate, but this one can be helpful. The Rocks and Waves model will further explain masculinity and femininity.

The masculine is the rocks. Strong. Solid. Order. Un-moving. Unchanging. It knows where it is and where it stands. It always points to the same truth. It is built upon a solid foundation (or it would have washed away long ago).

The feminine is the waves. Dynamic. Flowing. Surging. Bringing new life. Always changing. Providing beauty. Rocks alone are nowhere near as captivating without the waves.

The feminine flows in all directions with great power, surging with life and energy. The masculine builds canals, dams, and structures, bringing Order and safety. The contrast between the two builds differences (polarization) and helps define what they are. Waves without rocks are simply dull and predictable. You can find them in the middle of the ocean regularly. Rocks without waves are also boring. Nothing is happening. It might be pretty to look at for a bit, but one soon moves on to find something else.

The dance between the two is complicated, intricate, and constantly changing. The most significant growth of life is found where the waves and shore meet. Human cultures historically flourished here. (Look at most large cities today on a map; where are they?) We are drawn to these meeting places. The dance captivates and inspires us. The contrast helps define us and give us purpose. Life grows and flourishes here.

For a moment, consider the situation of a rock a bit deeper. Let us imagine one solitary rock doing its best to be a "good rock." He sits solid on the shore, minding his own business, when a feminine wave emerges and slaps him on the face.

"Hey, why did you do that? I was minding my own business!" he inquires of the wave.

The wave gives no response other than a few moments later to slap him again. As this continues, one might imagine his confusion growing. What has he done to deserve such abuse? He never did or said anything wrong, yet the assault is unending.

"It isn't just! It isn't fair! Leave me alone!" our poor rock cries out.

Yet, the worst possible outcome is for the rock to get what he wants. If he were moved away from the life-giving source of the ocean, what would his purpose be? A rock in the desert doesn't contribute anything to the growth and change of the world. This rock must wonder what a "good rock" actually wants and pursues.

The proper challenge to this confused rock is to lean into his role. Instead of merely "resisting" the feminine, what if he reshapes himself to "channel" the wave's energy into being productive? When shaped, rock can become an aqueduct, a power plant, or a shelter. Through sacrifice and hard work, he can extend the life-giving capacity of the wave further than it can reach on its own. He can build a legacy that will reach the future—providing shelter, safety, and support for future generations.

I invite you, as a man, to stop fearing and opposing the nature of the feminine. From the beginning, God created women to be the source of new life and potential. You can see the elemental surges of life built into her core biology. You can oppose and resist that energy, or you can channel it. If you demand that your wife make more sense, have more Order, and "be more like a rock" herself—you might get what you ask for.

Such would be a horrid outcome! There may be more peace (though likely not, given that she lives inconsistently with her true self). Still, there will undoubtedly be less attraction, energy, and life. Two rocks do not create an environment suited to growth and development.

Remember that the nature of the feminine appears opposed to the masculine. It is easy to claim that feminine interaction is painful and intrusive (it often is!) and resist it entirely.

The powerful Catholic man will, instead, channel this energy. He'll invite it even more strongly by using his Order to create safe and well-thought-out pathways for feminine energy. He knows that even though the wave may hurt when it slaps his face, it's part of a process that, if harnessed, will create a more robust, safer, and more life-giving home for his children. The hard work to be done is upon him. How does he shape and forge himself to guide this feminine energy?

Let's return to Ted and Emily. There are several ways Ted could have been a better "rock":

- Ted is not a slave to his job. Sometimes, a good rock says "no" and leans into the confrontation for the greater good. Ted will be married to Emily for his whole life. He'll get a new boss and even a new job regularly. If this was important for their relationship, Ted needs to be solid and strong enough to risk disappointing his boss.

- Ted likely knew about Emily's sensitivity to being late. With masculine responsibility and direction, Ted could have gotten ahead of the coming storm on his way home.

- When Ted first confronted Emily's anger, he could have taken responsibility and tried to meet her disappointment rather than dismissing her feelings. He could have steered that energy into a new plan. He might even have tried connective physical contact (e.g. holding her hand).

  Even as things escalated, Ted always had the option to take responsibility for his own shortcomings instead of blaming her. When he blamed her, he effectively asked her to be the "rock" in the relationship. This did not end well.

What would I tell Ted to do next time? Assuming the work request was genuinely important, Ted could have called, or at least sent a text, to guide Emily while also validating her feelings.

"Honey, I'm so sorry, there was a last-minute emergency at work, and I'm going to be a few minutes late. I understand if you are frustrated and embarrassed about being late, but I think we might still make it. Could you be my superhero and try to get everything ready? If we take off immediately, we might still make it! Either way, you're more important to me than anything at this party!"

Do you see the contrast? He's taking responsibility and making a plan. He's not only validating her negative feelings but also inviting a surge of positive feelings. If Ted steers the wave, good things are way more likely! There's no guarantee she will follow; with all our modern technology, we cannot control the sea. However, we can take responsibility as men for our contributions and work to improve things!

CHAPTER THREE
ORDER AND CHAOS

In ancient philosophy, Order was associated with masculinity, while Chaos was associated with femininity. This connection is found in multiple religious frameworks. It's a truth that transcends any individual teaching.

At first glance, this may seem unfair or unkind to the women. Many women may object to being associated with Chaos, and many men may prematurely celebrate without understanding. When explored properly, Order and Chaos offer powerful insights.

This model takes the rocks and waves to a deeper, more philosophical level. When this book becomes practical (and it will be painfully so!), I hope this model will help you understand why I am asking such difficult tasks of you as a man.

Order is "masculine"—and is very good. Order starts with the rocks but extends so much further. Order is the rules and systems of societies. It is the hierarchies, the safeguards, and the distribution systems that make everything work. It is the dependability of food to be in the supermarket. It assures a fair trial if you are taken to court. It is what allows us to sleep at night without worry.

Ultimately, Order becomes its enemy. One downside of our ultra-comfortable, safe, and secure society is that we have lost touch with the truth that God alone provides for our needs. We have pridefully become complacent in our self-reliance. How many men trust our 401(k) or investments to keep us safe? The words of Our Lord could not be clearer about placing our trust in the size of our barns.

Chaos is "feminine"—and is also very good. Chaos injects novelty, adaptation, and adventure. Chaos is the dragon's cave; it is risky, but it contains what men most want. If you risk engaging the dragon, you may win gold and a virgin! Without Chaos, an over-ordered society stagnates and calcifies. Chaos brings the spice of life and meaning and purpose. It is a faster heart rate as your fingers rub against those of your date while holding a glass of wine. It ultimately is the bringer of new life, experiences, and novelty. Nothing new comes from Order. We humans need novelty.

Chaos can also, in excess, become destructive. Change that is too fast, poorly considered, or reckless can bring destruction as surely as excessive Order. Many of the worst political atrocities come when Order has been rejected in favor of a new and exciting philosophy. Consider the story of Venezuela: it went from a booming first-world economy to poverty in just a few years by changing too much and too fast. Without constraint, Chaos ceases to be life-giving and becomes life-taking. You can see this even in the waves—giant waves we have no shelter from will kill us.

Both Order and Chaos are essential for humans. As much as this might seem contradictory, it is undeniable. Perhaps this shouldn't be surprising. My house needs heating in the winter and cooling in the summer. We fast on Good Friday, then feast on Easter. Humans need opposites. We all need both masculine and feminine energy at times.

While both are essential, they are not required *at the same time*. Imagine you are a pilgrim landing in the New World. Your need for Order is very high! You already have plenty of Chaos. You will first build houses, boats, weapons, and whatever you need to survive. All effort is devoted to this! Husbands and wives are not planning date nights when they're worried their family might die.

Life begins to simplify as this new society builds structures, rules, and procedures. In time, they may even start to get bored. Life seems flatter, plainer. Now is the time to plan a celebration or event! As Order continues to increase, Chaos becomes tolerable and highly desirable!

Your capacity to support life-giving Chaos depends on the quality of your Order. A well-ordered man with a properly structured life can support a lot of Chaos and even thrive in it. Feeling safe and protected, his wife will feel free to bring her feminine energy into the relationship fully. This mutual dynamic fulfills them and brings meaning, purpose, and satisfaction. You have probably experienced moments of this in your life.

Satisfaction is not found merely in perfect Order and Chaos but in every step towards that goal. Each time we improve ourselves, we feel satisfied and happy. You don't need to be perfect—you merely need to make one next step.

Imagine some children who want to play a game in this pilgrim village. At first, fear of being eaten by bears or wolves might prevent them from going outside their houses. After a wall has been built, the kids can play freely anywhere in the village; their capacity for safe Chaos is increased. When the dangerous wild animals are pushed back, the kids can play in the woods, too! As the village gets better food systems, the kids can play longer and spend less time working. Each increase in Order enables an increase in life-giving and fun Chaos. The adults experience this also. When they're not worried about getting enough food to survive, the adult parents can plan a date night and enjoy their interactions!

Let's be very careful not to confuse "male" with "masculine/ Order" or "female" with "feminine/Chaos." Both men and women can act from a masculine or feminine source. Our temperament (the natural viewpoint we have of the world) and upbringing affect this balance significantly. Consider temperaments; many people have heard of "Type A" vs. "Type B" people, but better assessments exist. The Big Five assessment is a more comprehensive assessment of temperament that captures many more parameters and shows a prominent and influential effect of gender.

A "masculine" temperament is less compliant (technically "disagreeable") and less sensitive to negative emotion (less "neurotic"). A feminine temperament is more compliant and more sensitive to negative emotions. These differences quickly make sense because caring for infants is a task that falls primarily on women. An infant needs tremendous support and is extremely fragile. These temperament differences appear to be custom-designed by God to help women care for infants. By contrast, men must confront the world and its harshness. The masculine temperament aids him with those tasks.

There are plenty of women with a masculine temperament and men with a feminine temperament. These people are not doomed to unsatisfying relationships. A highly agreeable and sensitive man can still find a way to be very masculine with his wife, but it may be more challenging. A very disagreeable and decisive woman can still be feminine with her husband, but it may take more effort.

If you find yourself in one of these situations, remember the power of the polarization model on attraction. You do want attraction in your marriage. Without it, things get sour fast.

There is much more to masculinity than a masculine temperament. We do not yet have all the psychological terminology to define masculinity fully. Still, I'll explain more in the next chapter.

For now, I want you to see that masculinity and femininity are not merely what men and women "should do." Instead, they are perspectives that men and women must work to put on when in an intimate relationship. Often, women in the workplace need to adopt a more masculine perspective, and men may need a more feminine perspective to deal with their young children.

Let me give one practical example to help shape this. Father Michael Schmitz teaches an elegant concept highlighting the difference between masculine and feminine as they love their children. He claims that mothers tend to have "present" love for their children, while fathers tend to have "future" love. Let me explain this with an example.

Let's pretend young Billy rides his bicycle down a dangerous dirt hill with a cliff at the bottom. On the way down, he loses control and wipes out. He is bleeding from several cuts and is pretty upset but has no broken bones or other significant injuries. Consider the reactions of mom and dad when he gets home:

Mom: "Oh, Billy, are you okay? What do you need? Can I get you a Band-Aid and some ice? Do you need to go to the doctor? Sit down, rest, and I'll get everything you need!"

Dad: "Billy, what were you thinking!!? That's so dangerous to go down that hill. You've been told multiple times not to go there and to be safe. You are grounded for a week!"

In this scenario, Mom often gets upset, thinking that Dad doesn't love young Billy. In reality, Dad correctly sees that high-risk and dangerous behavior can potentially hurt Billy in the future. He loves Billy so much that he doesn't want to see him destroy himself down the road.

Dad loves Billy's future self—Dad is terrified that Billy needs a wake-up call to be safe.

Mom is also correct. Billy is having a tough time and is hurting right now. He has actual physical needs that do need tending right now. Her maternal instincts have activated, and she wants to nurture her baby!

Suppose this couple discusses this concept outside of the situation. In that case, Mom and Dad can relate better and work together as a team when a disaster happens. But let's go deeper. Consider these two reactions from the perspectives of masculine and feminine.

Dad's response is one of Order. The systems that keep kids safe have broken. Broken systems are terrifying for the masculine! The waves and tides of the Chaos of the world may sweep in and cause immense damage. Dad knows that Billy needs Order of his own to succeed later in life. He addresses the most significant danger he sees; Billy survived this incident but may not survive the next time the systems fail.

Mom's response is that of Chaos. At this moment, her waves have surged hard into big feelings. The waves live in the now. They have swirled around a hurt child who needs care. To the feminine, the future is often less important than the significant needs of the present. It's not that she doesn't care about future Billy; it's more that she cannot see that right now. In the spray of the waves, all she can see is Billy's pain now.

God designed these two perspectives to be complementary. They're both right, and they're both needed. The marital conflict that often arises in this situation stems not from malice or ill will, but rather from a difference in perspective.

As the man, the source of Order, it is your job to build the systems, even within your marital plan, for disciplining children to bridge this gap. If you've ever had an event like this end in a big fight with your wife, it's your job to help repair the damage done. Do it smartly! Choose a good time in a moment outside of stress. Present it in a way that invites her to join you in loving Billy, not in a way that makes her look wrong. Consider using a reference like Father Mike in your explanation.

You must bring the Order and the systems. If you delay and wait for her to do it, she shifts out of her feminine and into a masculine state. This shift not only weakens attraction but also breaks your mutual marital identities. If she is masculine, why does she need you? Particularly if she is hurt and upset, it is tough to find a connection when she is required to be masculine.

We need one final addition to the model of Order and Chaos. While I have tried to describe how each can be good, each has a toxic version. Our world has many examples of both toxic Order and toxic Chaos. Many of the struggles people have in understanding and embracing their roles as men and women are due to the many abuses that have occurred through these toxic versions. One of the goals of this book is to help you identify the difference.

CHAPTER FOUR
MASCULINITY BASICS

Using these models, I will focus on a positive view of masculinity from a Catholic perspective. The world screams about the dangers of "toxic masculinity" yet rarely considers the positive power. I will describe aspects of masculinity that, when embraced, result in a powerful and very positive masculine force. Masculinity is dangerous. However, it becomes a powerful protector when pointed in a safe direction.

SUBMITS TO AUTHORITY

A good rock understands that it is part of something larger than itself. A rock floating free is merely an asteroid—it doesn't do any good and is a far greater potential danger. When a rock is subordinated to a larger structure (say, the earth below it), it gains solidness and the capacity to be a source of strength for others. All too often, men want to be a one-man show. We want to be Indiana Jones, submitting to no one. The bodies crushed in the wake of such men tell their own stories.

Similarly, Order can only reach its potential if it submits to a higher Order. Biology must obey the laws of Chemistry, and Chemistry must obey those of Physics, and so on. So, too, a man must obey a proper Order: his Father, community, state, country, etc.

Of course, God is the ultimate authority. Only when a man's authority is structured correctly can he truly express his maximum potential for good. Relying on oneself or going alone is ultimately to fail as a man.

I struggle with this regularly. For example, I had a disagreement with my parish priest when my third child was ready to receive communion. I pushed back pretty hard, ultimately damaging my relationship with him while not getting the kiddo communion any faster. He had legitimate authority in this domain; my proper place was to submit.

RESISTS THE STORM

A rock provides shelter for those who need it. When the floods, winds, and rain come, wise people naturally seek refuge on the rock, not the sand. A good rock, grounded in authority, also provides shelter in opposition to the storm of the world. A man must make space within his shelter for those he loves and those he is charged to care for (not always the same list). A man must sacrifice, often hollowing out part of himself he might not otherwise wish to. A rock that gives no shelter or providence is useless.

Similarly, Order must stand as a bulwark against toxic Chaos. Not all Chaos is life-giving and good. There is toxic femininity and toxic Chaos aplenty in our world. In the Garden of Eden, Eve was confronted with toxic Chaos in the form of the serpent. It was Adam's job to protect from that storm, too. He was there, silent and inactive, as the serpent seduced his wife. He should have confronted the serpent and risked upsetting Eve. Instead, he chose comfort and failed her.

Today's world is filled with many forms of toxic Order and toxic Chaos. Dark forces seek to corrupt and consume our children, our Faith, our resources, and our families. We do not live in a moral age, and we do not have virtuous leaders. Like the serpent in the garden, this darkness has targeted those we love. We must become a rock that shelters our loved ones. This transformation will come at a cost, and it will be painful.

PREDICTABLE AND DEPENDABLE

A man honors his word. Rocks do not suddenly become playdough—at least not unless something terrible has happened. We build structures out of rock and depend on them to function and continue to work. We know how rock works—how to shape, use, and preserve it. To be a good rock means we cannot give in to whimsy and fickle desire. We must make and honor our commitments. When a man makes a vow, he holds his life in his own hands.

Order can only continue being orderly if it maintains its identity. Indeed, a description of something that was once orderly but changed unpredictably is "chaotic." Masculinity needs predictability and dependability by definition. To violate our word is to diminish ourselves. Femininity is not affected in the same way. A man must keep his word, at least to the best of his abilities (and we know internally the difference between a real emergency and a pathetic excuse to avoid).

Consider the role of a politician as an example. According to the concept of a representative democracy, we choose one representative who travels to the government center to "represent" us. Suppose this individual is inconsistent and does not honor his word; destructive Chaos results. The system becomes unstable. Votes swing for power and money rather than virtue and honesty. Does this result sound familiar?

The first time I met my friend, Travis, he invited me to take some kids camping with him. While following him into the Idaho wilderness, his trailer blew a tire. After pulling over, he strongly encouraged me to keep going but gave me only vague directions to the "spot." He assured me, however, that he would be there no matter what.

I took my best guess and thought I found the spot. Five hours later, however, he hadn't arrived. I put the kids to bed with a sinking feeling that this would be a solo trip. Just a few minutes later, however, Travis pulled in. The flat tire was only the beginning of his many problems, but he had told me he would be there and wanted to honor his word.

Travis encountered many vehicle breakdowns that day and found very little help. He had solid justification to give up on the camping trip and return home. His persistence proved to be an indication of his character that I will never forget. There's a lot of wilderness in Idaho that has no cellphone coverage. Travis is one of the few men I trust when it comes to going in deep.

INTENTIONAL VS REACTIVE

When a wave crashes into a shore, it reacts to what is there. Chaos is the essence of flow, of energy, of unpredictability. Femininity reacts to the Order that masculinity creates.

You see this dramatically when watching a skilled dancing pair. We are mesmerized when a skilled male dancer leads a skilled female dancer. He creates a plan with intentional moves to position himself and herself as the dance progresses. He creates and executes a plan for them both to follow.

She, by contrast, merely reacts to his lead. She begins a spin when his hand goes up and to the left. When it drops and wraps around her, she moves in close. A slight pressure to the left leads her to move in that direction. It almost seems both dancers scripted it beforehand—but this is not true. Her reaction in following is so precise that the slightest cue is sufficient to keep them aligned.

What's fascinating about watching this dancing pair is how each thrills and delights in their roles. Women are deeply pleased to follow a male who properly leads them. They are not bitter and resentful about having to follow the orders of a man but instead revel and delight in the freedom of simply being, simply feeling the energy of the dance.

By contrast, the man does not view it as a burden or obligation to plan and execute. He delights in and relishes the incredible feeling of power and control as this beautiful woman submits to his cues. This mutual enjoyment is not an indicator of toxic masculinity or male domination; instead, this is each gender living into their God-designed roles and finding the peace and fulfillment we all find when we align our will to God's.

A healthy masculinity must embrace the task of being intentional. Sometimes, this is hard, and often, it is inconvenient. We often do not "feel" like doing it. Such feelings must not sway a man who wants to be a powerful force for good (he is not to be Chaos!); he must lean into his dependable foundation status and be intentional in his actions.

I worked with a man once whose wife wanted him to be in charge of the finances. He wasn't naturally inclined to pay attention to financial details, so this was a challenge. He reacted to her complaints for years by attempting to "do better." These efforts were frustrating to both spouses.

I challenged him to identify what he believed was his proper role in financial management for his household. Rather than merely reacting to his wife's complaints, he could create a plan he genuinely believed in and then lead her down that plan. While it was still a work in progress, the tone of the engagement was very different. His wife, while she did not get everything she wanted, really appreciated his initiative and leadership.

DECISIVE

To "decide" something is literally to "kill off" the other options. It shares a common root with words like "regicide" or "homicide." Decide is not a word or concept that is subtle or lightly undertaken. It's not necessarily bad (though there are indeed bad decisions), but it must be weighed and considered appropriately.

The heart of the feminine does not like to kill things. It is the job of Order to do the killing. We men kill an animal or a plant to provide food. We eliminate the Chaos of our environments to forge and create a home and a place of safety. It is the job of Chaos to surge in after the killing is done and fill the space with life and growth.

When we build an aqueduct to distribute water, we choose a single design, killing off all the other paths the water might flow. When we marry our wives, we kill off all the alternate marriage options for both parties. When we choose to move from one city to another, we kill off all the potential that might have occurred if we stayed.

I do not mean that women are incapable of making decisions—not at all. First, women can act out of a masculine energy when decisions need to be made. Second, they have a more feminine way; most women like to make decisions as part of a group. You'll often see a group of women collect, talk (a lot), and ultimately come to a group decision. They usually announce it using group language, e.g., "We decided..."

By contrast, men tend to decide on their own. They collect information from many sources, including men and women they trust. The final decision, however, is made by himself. He binds his will to the act of killing the other options. Order cannot exist with ambiguous possibilities. Order must have clear "yes" and "no" decisions regularly. A man who leans into his masculinity must be decisive.

Some who believe all masculinity is toxic may, at this point, accuse me of making women out to be mindless slaves. Not true at all! Women frequently and wisely make decisions. Consider, however, the size of what is being "killed." If she decides to make hamburgers for dinner, the version of dinner that was spaghetti is killed off. An alternate meal plan is a pretty minor death and does not greatly conflict with her femininity.

Furthermore, when a woman manages her family, she often acts out of a masculine role. In that role, she may make significant decisions. However, be cautious about asking her to take on that role when you're seeking mutual attraction and chemistry.

A man can greatly bless his woman by making the big decisions and allowing his woman to fill in the gaps. For example, he might announce that they are going out on a date night (killing off some of the savings and other possible evening activities) and then solicit her input on what type of food she desires. He can further bless her femininity by choosing a restaurant that aligns with her desires.

For a bonus, he can sometimes even sneak information out of her without her realizing it. For example, he might say, "Tonight we're going out! I'm taking you to that restaurant you said you were really excited about!" He may have forgotten what it was, but she hasn't! She feels safe and secure when he makes decisions while considering her needs. She likely doesn't feel she has to kill anything off. She's free to surge in excitement without risk. She's free to be feminine.

Some time ago, I attempted to take my wife out on a date while trying a very restrictive diet. I didn't have any good options for where to eat that would work with this diet, so I was indecisive about where to go. I asked her what she wanted and if she preferred restaurants A, B, or C. This passiveness was poorly received. She got frustrated!

I realized that part of the fun of the date for her is the freedom from making decisions and being allowed to flow and enjoy the time. My persisting questions were transforming the event from an enjoyable date into work. She asked me to choose somewhere I'd enjoy going, even if I wasn't planning to eat anything. I realized that asking her to make those decisions pushed her out of her feminine.

DEFEND THE WEAK

I enjoy going to the gym and doing CrossFit. I'm strong and can lift and move significant weights. I recently had a fun conversation with several men who work out; interestingly, we all shared a secret dream. We each would love to be strong enough in an emergency to save others. This desire is not unique to CrossFit folk.

Rocks must be strong—strong enough to impose the Order they want to represent (a Christian moral system in our case) upon the world. Sometimes, this Order is opposed by others, all too often when they are seeking an immoral goal. Setting your strength against those acting immorally is called "defending the weak."

It is baked into every man's biology to want to defend those who cannot. This feeling is enshrined and dramatized throughout the many superhero movies. We glorify soldiers who sacrifice themselves to save others. These stories are so popular because they appeal to something deep and powerful.

Order is most noble and true when it protects those who need protection. A good rock does not merely protect itself, but it also provides shelter for those who need it. As a man growing in positive masculinity, seek those who would benefit from your defense. Commonly, you can start at home; your wife and children need you to defend them from the forces of evil that control the world. Also, around your workplace, community, and other areas. A meek man (more on that word later) will be able to be led by God to find those whom God is calling him to defend.

One more note on defending: You must be dangerous to oppose those who are dangerous. Imagine a sheepdog defending his sheep. When the wolves come, the sheepdog must be strong, well-trained, and disciplined enough to defeat them. Defending the weak does not mean becoming weak but rather becoming very strong and dangerous. Then, point yourself in the right moral direction.

One time, I took a big group of kids to a fair in town. After looking at the animals, we went to this hay maze, which was pretty cool. I let the kids run through it while checking my email. A minute later, however, my oldest ran to me, asking for my help. She said a boy was hurting a younger girl, and it wasn't right.

I ran after her to see what was up, and she was correct. This young boy was hitting, pinching, and kicking this girl who seemed like she might be his sister. Several other adults in the area were pretending not to notice while the little girl cringed and cried. I could not stand by idly.

While keeping my hands visible, I wrapped my arms widely around the boy, creating a fence with them. The girl was free to back up, while all the boy could do was hit my arms. I told him firmly, "Young man, it is not appropriate to hit other kids like this." After several attempts to get free, he calmed down a bit. A few minutes later, the adults in charge of these children returned and took over.

As the struggling family walked away, several mothers thanked me for helping the little girl. One man, however, looked down at his feet and wouldn't make eye contact with me. We live in an age where adults must be extremely careful around children. I assumed he was blaming me, but I later realized he felt ashamed. He had been there longer than I had but had taken no action. Men are meant to defend the weak. When we do not, we are diminished.

Yes, I took a risk in publicly restricting a child who was not my responsibility. This other man, however, took a different type of risk. He has to live with himself, knowing that he made himself to be the type of man who would watch a young girl be hurt and not take any action.

PROVIDE

Providing was a pretty straightforward (though challenging) aspect of masculinity for most of history. Modern culture has thrown us some big curveballs. Here are some important elements of "providing" in the 21st century:

- To provide is not necessarily to grow the crops yourself. It is to make sure your family is provided for. For many families, this means the wife may have to engage in some amount of work. Your wife having to work is not optimal—especially if younger children are at home. We make the best of the times we live in. If possible, make a plan so she can one day be home with the children. Work as hard as possible, and surrender the rest to the Lord.

- It ought to be possible for a man to work hard and provide a reasonable income for his family. Many political factors have resulted in damaging decisions that have deflated the currency and radically increased the cost of living beyond what many reasonable jobs provide. Our response is not to complain, extort, or manipulate others but to trust in God.

  I know many families that struggle to make ends meet. Consider looking for a new job or multiple jobs. Consider other alternatives. But above all, trust that God has a plan, that it is a good plan, and it is right for you. God will provide. Do your best, and trust Him with the rest.

- It is sadly no longer the case that working hard and being honorable is enough to keep a good job. Leftist agendas have taken over our workplaces, and many men today face tough choices about what they choose to say if they want to keep their jobs. Never compromise your faith or integrity. If you go down that path, you will lose far more than any job is worth.

  Read the stories from the Bible (e.g., Maccabees) to find inspiration. There are times when some men are called to become martyrs. Today, the most common American martyr may be the man who loses his job for his faith. If you are pondering if this might be your time, go to Confession and spend significant time in prayer. Consult other men you trust and respect. Ultimately, be completely submissive to God's will. There is no virtue in making a sacrifice you are not called to—but do not compromise yourself.

- Never let your faith be in the size of your "barns." Read Luke 12:13-21 if you need help remembering the parable. Throughout time, most people have innately understood the balance between what I do and what God does. When a farmer planted his fields, watered the crops, and spread the manure, he would work as hard as possible. However, he was under no illusion that his efforts would guarantee success. He knew that God would bless his work with rain, protect his crop from damaging pests, and cause the plants to grow abundantly at His will.

  The ancient code is *Ora et Labora*, Pray and Work. It is your job to work hard to provide. Never forget that God provides the actual things. Pray first. Then, work hard. Finally, trust Him. His plan is always best.

- There is a crisis of men who remain boys currently going on in our culture. More and more men have graduated from High School or college, then perhaps overwhelmed by the vicious attacks of the culture, retreat home again to their parents' basement. Hiding is not what God intended (at least not as a general rule.)

Instead, all too often, this comes from a combination of fear of not being good enough combined with unwillingness to pick up a heavy responsibility. Like a timid high school boy standing on the side of the ballroom, too afraid to ask a pretty girl to actually dance with him, these young men are unwillingly missing the real adventure to hold onto an illusion of safety.

God does not create "junk." God does not set us up for failure. If you are in this situation, I invite you to make a radical change. Embrace the responsibility. Pick up the heaviest burden you can, carry it as long as possible, and then look for a bigger one. It is how we prove to ourselves that we are becoming men—not by the outcome, but by the effort. It's all we can control anyway. The rest is in God's hands. Trust Him.

LEAD AND GO FIRST

Imagine a harsh army drill sergeant barking orders to his raw cadets. An image from a movie might come to your mind. *"Drop and give me fifty, maggot!"* If this is your idea of leadership, you likely want to avoid becoming a leader.

What if there were a different vision you could embrace for leadership? What if leadership looked a lot more like Christ than the drill sergeant? When Christ washed the apostles' feet, He invited them to do the same as future church leaders. I invite you to a Christ-like vision of masculine leadership, a more profound and sacrificial service.

I wonder if one reason the world is so afraid of masculine leadership is that it fears the drill sergeant and doesn't know or trust Christ. When a man leads from a place of serving, everything changes. When he places the good of those he is in charge of above his own good, others want to follow him.

While few current political leaders lead this way, we have better historical examples. Imagine the elected president choosing his primary opponent to be his vice president. He then proceeds to fill his cabinet with people who disagree with him. Sounds crazy, right? That's what Abraham Lincoln did—not for appearances but because he genuinely believed it was the best way to serve the people he was elected to lead.

Sometimes, God calls us to lead those we love into a scary place. I know of many men who, in this current political time, have been called to leave their corporate jobs due to moral or ethical disagreements. Losing an established and comfortable income can be terrifying for a wife! In these situations, we men must lead even more boldly. If you know your family's income is decreasing, be the first to reduce your spending. It's easy to justify our expenses as "necessary" when they aren't. Take the first step into pain. Don't ask your wife and children (or those who report to you at work) to go into a difficult place you are unwilling to. Take the first step.

During the D-Day landing, there is a story of one particular sergeant in charge of a boatload of terrified Marines. Standing in front of them, in a loud and commanding voice, he said, *"Men, my boots will be the first to hit this sand. They will stay on the sand as long as any of you. They will be the very last to leave this sand."* This man knew how to lead! He took the first step and served his men well. Be a service-based leader who is willing to go first. If you need more help with this concept, I recommend John Maxwell, an author who explores this idea in great detail in many books.

CHALLENGE

What does it matter if you were to build a fantastic aqueduct system but never actually ran the water? The quality of the Order imposed is only genuinely found by being challenged with a bit of Chaos. Without that challenge, the best you have is simply a good plan for the future.

This limitation brings up one critical difference between men and women that often goes unnoticed. Masculinity requires challenges to thrive. Femininity does not. This difference has several practical consequences:

- Other men are helping you when they challenge you, even in public. It may feel a bit embarrassing for your so-called friends to call you out in a humorous way (at least to them) in front of a crowd. To insecure men, this may feel like an attack. It isn't. Suppose you are not strong enough to handle the tiny bit of Chaos from your buddies' well-intentioned slights. In that case, you are not ready to handle the far greater Chaos of life and femininity. This challenge is part of the growth process!

  Consider the Proverbs: "As iron sharpens iron, so one man sharpens another." Have you ever rubbed two pieces of iron together? The closest typical example is using a grinding wheel. It's very good at sharpening, but it's a hot, painful, and even damaging process. You want other men to sharpen you; you likely will only sometimes enjoy it.

- Men are complimenting you when they challenge you. Most men do intend well when they launch these small slights and insults. You probably know a few men who are too weak and fragile to handle these challenges well.

  If you look closely, other men tend to stop challenging these fragile ones. Why? Because the other men know the fragile ones aren't strong enough to handle it. They are not likely to respect the weaker men either.

By contrast, we challenge those we men know can handle it. View these challenges as a statement that "you are capable and strong!" It's a signal to other men who may not know you as well that you are a good man. This signaling is one way men communicate. It's not some macho-man thing; it's living into the nature of masculinity. The power of our Order is only revealed when tested by a bit of Chaos. These other men are confident in your Order. That's a powerful compliment!

- Challenge brings humility to men. The best response to a challenge is to roll with it and simultaneously ponder if something at the root needs addressing. Pride is the most deadly of sins partly because it is the sneakiest. Let me explain. No man wakes up in the bed of another woman and wonders if he's guilty of lust—similarly, the morning after a drinking binge leaves little doubt if gluttony has occurred. Pride, however, by its very nature, justifies and obscures itself. Having other men you respect and care for to help you see yourself better is a great blessing. This process may seem harsh initially, but it is worth it.

- Be wary if the men in your life are not challenging you. It could mean several things: First, perhaps they're not masculine. Find new friends. Alternatively, they might believe you're too weak to handle it. This scenario is particularly likely if you see them challenging most other men. If this might be the case, it's time to make a change.

Gird your loins and ask them confidentially why they don't challenge you. If you have behaved poorly, admit it and take responsibility for it. Then, commit to trying to do better and ask for their help.

RESPONSIBILITY

Several books have recently been published about taking responsibility. Whether by David Goggins or Jocko Willink, they contain similar themes about the importance of acting as if every outcome depends upon us. These ideas work; many people find them effective and empowering, improving their lives.

As Catholics, however, we must acknowledge that God alone is ultimately responsible for all outcomes. Isaiah 7 and 14 tell us that God is the ultimate authority on earth. This idea has many more references, but the conclusion is unavoidable: God must be acknowledged as ultimately responsible for everything. How, then, do we understand the concepts of these modern authors?

I propose that Goggins, Willink, and others' work is a form of "model," as I define it here. It's not true, but it is helpful. While extreme ownership is a relatively simple model, it lacks some qualities that a Catholic man must also hold: faith and trust in the Lord.

A Catholic man must be able to hold two conflicting truths that sometimes seem to be contradictory. Yes, God is ultimately in charge of all outcomes and results. Yet, at the same time, it is often beneficial if we take responsibility anyway. Threading between these is the art of Christian masculine responsibility.

I want to consider the benefits of the "extreme ownership" model from a Catholic perspective. God created us in His "image and likeness." This gift means, to a lesser extent, we have creative power—not that of God's but more so than the rest of worldly creation. This creative power is most true over ourselves. Early Church Fathers taught that we "give birth" to our future selves. Based on the choices we make, we become what we choose. If I engage in lust, I become a lustful man. If I decide to pursue gentleness, I become a gentleman.

Our creative power is not limited to ourselves. As men, we can call forth the goodness in others. I address this further in Chapter 7. Most obviously, we have the power to take the goods that God has created (e.g., wood, stone, metal) and create complex goods. This creative power is real.

This creative power need not be used for good. When I insult my children, smash my worldly goods, or engage in sinful behavior, I bring darkness into the world. Worse yet, my prideful nature does not want to see this darkness, let alone take responsibility for my actions. I'd rather blame God, as He is said to be ultimately responsible anyway.

We humans actually enjoy blaming, complaining, and grumbling. It may not be obvious, but it feels good to complain or blame someone else. It means I don't have to look at my shortcomings and failings. I don't have to be responsible for fixing the problem. It is much easier to sit back, crack open a cold beer, and let someone else do the work.

Many times in the Bible, God punishes the Israelites when they complain and blame Him. It consistently seems that God believes it is wrong to do this. One reason is our fallen human nature. We are so eager to excuse and forgive ourselves that complaining and blaming are too much to bear.

There's a similar reason why modesty is so important. We men are sinful, and the temptations of the flesh are often just too much to bear. It is critical for men to avoid inappropriate views of the female body, not because the female body is bad—but because we cannot handle the beauty. The risk of sin is so significant.

Similarly, as humans, our desire not to be responsible for our sins is too great to allow blame and complaining. Out of vice, especially pride, we are desperate to maintain the illusion that we aren't quite as responsible as we are for the darkness we have brought. We want to hide from this truth.

When we "accept responsibility" or take "extreme ownership," we must acknowledge that we did things poorly or even wrong. It pulls the prideful lie away, exposing the seemingly inevitable misstep. Whether an immoral action or merely a mistake, there is almost always something we could have done better. Our odds of finding it on our own are low.

Next, consider the implications of God's ultimate responsibility. There are two forms of "God's will:" His "active" will and His "passive" will. The active will is what He directly causes to bring about. For example, He created the world in 6 days through active steps. By contrast, God allows many things by His passive will. He allowed Hitler to rise to power and kill millions of Jews. We do not know why or what good God has brought to pass, but we believe in His goodness!

Our perspectives change once we realize that every occurrence in the universe must occur either by God's active will or by God's passive will. If I sin and make a mistake, God may allow it, but only when He can bring about a greater good. I can trust with absolute confidence that He has a plan to bring about the greatest possible good—especially when I cannot see it.

Imagine a farmer before the Industrial Revolution. He knows that he must work hard—till the fields, plant the crops, fertilize, water, etc. No matter how hard and long he labors, he still knows that, ultimately, the crop depends upon God. He certainly will keep a mental record of what works better or worse. He will learn from his mistakes. He will spend his blood and sweat to provide for his family. But he will never forget that God is completely in charge. We must do the same.

When I worked in the corporate world, I had a very comfortable income and a lot of really cool benefits. That's a big part of why I resisted leaving for so long when God called me to go. After leaving, everything seemed OK—at least for a while.

I'll never forget the month that my wife told me we didn't even have enough money to pay the bills.

I was angry with God—I had followed His direction; why had He allowed this to happen? I pushed, persuaded, and did what I could to sell more. We still weren't going to make it. I went to Adoration and simply prayed, asking God for help. The next day, we closed a sale that was just enough to cover that month's expenses. I thought maybe this was just a test I had to pass, but the next month was just as bad.

It was hard for me to work so hard and not see the money come in. After going through this dance enough times, however, it has gotten a little bit easier. Through these cycles, I've learned to keep working hard, especially when I feel helpless.

Take responsibility for the outcome, but trust God to make it happen!

CHAPTER FIVE
CHRIST'S MASCULINITY

Christ is supposed to be the ultimate role model for all who wear His name. Yet, so often, we fail not only to follow but also to recognize the model. In this chapter, I hope to extend the image of "What is Masculinity?" by appealing to the perfect man, Jesus Christ.

CHRIST WAS OBEDIENT

At first, this might seem obvious, but it needs some discussion. The question is, "What authority?" It's relatively simple to understand that a rock must submit to the immense authority of the earth underneath. We see that Christ was regularly obedient to God, even to the point of death, despite His desperate longing for a different plan in the Garden of Gethsemane.

As a Catholic man, you likely give intellectual assent to obeying God's laws. It's time to probe to see if that goes deeper—do you follow the laws of God and His Church even when they are painful or difficult? Have you broken the church's ban on Contraception? The majority of Catholics have. Do you surrender all parts of your bedroom life to His will? How about your bank account and your calendar? It's easy to surrender an hour on Sundays. It's much harder to give everything over.

Even if so, there is still more. Christ submitted to earthly powers as well; He was obedient to Rome. Consider the passage in Matthew 17:24-27 where Christ is challenged to pay the temple tax. Even though He identifies that they should be exempt, He arranges payment anyway. In a similar concept, He instructs us to "give to Caesar what is Caesar's" (see Matthew 22:21 for example). Why would He instruct His apostles to submit themselves to earthly authority?

This requirement is a difficult concept for Americans, in particular, to grapple with. Independence from government authority is a vital part of our founding story. Yet, the Romans were likely more oppressive to the Jews than the British were to the colonies. Why does Jesus call for obedience to a corrupt and abusive system?

The Catechism, starting in paragraph 2238, describes that we must obey earthly authorities for the Lord's sake. Many might jump directly to paragraph 2242, which explains that we must not obey authority when it issues an immoral order. Although immoral laws are becoming more common today, they do not justify disobedience to morally appropriate orders.

Finally, Christ was obedient to Mary and Joseph. Consider that for a moment. Christ is the Son of God—in every single way superior to both. Yet He humbled Himself and obeyed not only Mary (his biological mother) but even Joseph, who was not his biological Father. Christ shows that the office of Father and Mother, even when indirect, is worthy of obedience. What does this mean in practical language for us moderns? In-laws. Yep, we must be respectful and perhaps even obedient to the inlaw parents. While, of course, not in situations where they contradict our moral conscience, most of us should obey more.

Follow Christ's example. Unless there is a clear moral violation, obey. Also, that helps bring humility.

CHRIST WAS MEEK

It's funny that Christ uses few adjectives to describe Himself in the gospels. One of the clearest and strongest adjectives He uses for Himself is "meek." Check out Matthew 11:29 for an example. But what is meek?

Consider a wild stallion: strong, beautiful, independent. Imagine this horse, unrivaled power, dashing through the meadow. Beautiful? Yes, of course! But it's not very useful. Imagine this magnificent being captured by men and brought back to the stables. At first, this beast refuses the bridle and saddle. After time and training, the horse learns to accept these, and his great strength can now be used to do incredible things.

The stallion has become "meeked." He is as strong as ever, but now submits to external leadership and is fruitful. This process is what God wishes for all of us men.

The world attempts to limit the damage caused by masculinity by sabotaging men's strength and power. A weak man isn't a danger to anyone. But Christ was not weak. Instead, Christ invites us to become meek. Unlike the stallion described above, the Christian must submit himself, by his own volition, to the saddle, bridle, and yoke of those in authority. Doing so allows the great strength God has given us to be harnessed and channeled to create the good God intends.

Only a meek horse can make a big contribution to the world. Only a meek man can fully cooperate with God's plans. Do not become weak, but become meek. Surrender your pride and autonomy, and submit your will to the Lord. Accept his bridle.

CHRIST WAS DEPENDABLE

In the previous chapter, I spoke about how a man must honor his word. Christ certainly did that, but he did so much more. In the gospels, what could the disciples reliably depend upon Christ to do? He did not make every person happy or perform every desired miracle. He could have easily prevented Judas's or Peter's betrayals, but chose not to. Why?

We know Christ, being God's Son, was united perfectly with the Father. I claim we can depend on Christ to do what He believed the Father's will to be. If the Father wished for a miracle, Christ performed it. If the Father wished otherwise, Christ complied.

In a typical job, "dependable" means delivering your boss's desired results. In many marriages, "dependable" means reliably giving your wife what she wants. So often, we use something of the world to decide if we're being dependable—but this doesn't seem right.

Some desires require a violation of our integrity to be fulfilled. Imagine asking a rock to break into pieces so water could flow more easily. At first, this request may seem reasonable. Just a more complex aqueduct, yes? Yet, what has happened to the rock? Its very identity has changed. Its foundation is shifted. It is no longer the same type of rock as it used to be. It may be more work to redesign the river and move the rock without breaking it, but the resulting waterway will be stronger if done well.

God created each man uniquely and wonderfully. He does not want you to compromise yourself. Don't be confused—laundry, cleaning, or dishes are not a compromise; help your wife! If, however, she starts slandering someone, do not participate. Supporting her in a vice or even a mistake is not "being dependable."

Let me share a brief story of when I screwed this concept up badly. Several years ago, my wife wanted a new puppy. We had six little children, several new businesses we were trying to build, and an older house on 5 acres that required a lot of upkeep. I knew, deep, deep down, that this was not the time to get a puppy.

Oh, and she wanted a unique, special, high-energy border collie puppy, too.

I failed to speak the truth that I knew. My wife wanted the dog, so I caved and told her she could. Within days of bringing the dog home, it was clear this was a complete disaster. Household stress went through the roof! Poop, hair, chewed-up debris, band-aids on too-aggressive puppy nibbles, wasp stings (another story), and various other messes were frequent. The reign of terror culminated in the puppy's untimely demise as she finally caught a vehicle tire she loved to chase. The driver was faultless; the dog pulled away from my daughter and found a quick death under the tires. Our family was devastated; many tears flowed at the burial and prayers.

The following morning, before the crowning achievement of my immaturity, my wife confessed how much more peaceful and calm everything was with the dog's loss. Perhaps the dog truly was a mistake. Not only did I respond with the foolish, *"I told you so,"* but I even added, *"And that's why I can't depend upon you and your ideas!"* This response is one of many I wish I could redo.

Several days later, I related this story to my coach, who promptly stopped the story and challenged me.

"Michael, it's not your wife you can't depend on and trust; it's yourself."

"How does that make sense, coach? It was her idea!"

"It's very simple, Michael. You knew the right decision deep down. You knew it was your job to make that decision. You didn't. You failed yourself. You failed to fulfill the duty that God has given you. Like Adam in the Garden of Eden, you sat there and did nothing."

I was silenced. He was entirely right.

Christ is marvelously dependable, but He doesn't just give us what we want. Instead, we can depend on Him to do what is right even when, or perhaps especially when, it creates hardship for others.

Be dependable and do what is right. Pray and discern carefully to find the right path. Do not deviate, even if your family, kids, boss, in-laws, or anyone else wants you to! Follow the will of the Lord, especially when it is unpopular. It will not make friends— and probably will make enemies! Follow the example of Christ.

CHRIST WAS HUMBLE

It's often hard for men to ask for directions. Why? Do we think asking hurts us? Do we fear being judged as incompetent? Perhaps we fear rejection?

I submit to you that this behavior is simply due to pride. If you have never earnestly and slowly prayed the Litany of Humility, that's your homework. It's at the end of this book. It's a painful prayer to pray if we mean it! It changes our lives when we commit. So many men have this painfully wrong view that a man must be self-sufficient, like some modern John Wayne or Indiana Jones, to be worthy. We never measure up!

The irony is that the only man who was self-sufficient and worthy on His own merits asked for tons of help! This man was Christ, of course. He never actually needed help. Consider Matthew 26:53. With a single word, countless legions of Angels would appear on Christ's behalf. With His power, He could have instantly and forever changed anything in the world. There were and are no limits; Christ was, is, and ever will be able to do it all!

And yet, He outsourced so many tasks to his apostles. Why? It's not like they were particularly skilled or capable at the jobs He gave them. They generally screwed things up! So why would Christ ask them for help?

Perhaps you've watched your wife invite one of the young children into the kitchen to help "cook the meal." If you watch closely, you'll quickly notice the child isn't helping. They generally make things more difficult. Why does your wife do this? It makes no sense from an engineering perspective; it's simply a waste of time and resources!

Yet, if you are willing to look at this situation from the perspective of God, it becomes a beautiful scene. Both the woman and the child benefit from this interaction. The mother experiences the child's joy and love. The child thrives in the attention and opportunity offered by the mother. Both gain far more than they lose.

Christ allowed others to help Him not for His benefit but for theirs! He was humble enough to ask for help as a gift to others. That gift multiplied exponentially as the apostles followed in His example.

I invite you to a deeper humility in your life. Think less of yourself and what you want. When we become more humble, everyone benefits. Pray the Litany of Humility regularly. Surrender your sense of how things should be and accept that of the Lord instead.

CHRIST WAS EMOTIONALLY SOLID

I've invented the term "emotionally solid," so don't look for it in the Bible. Let me define it and then show how Christ fulfilled it (and why it matters!).

To be a rock-like man requires a solid and firm foundation in all the dimensions of humanity, including emotions. He isn't crushed and swayed by them. The ocean surges in response to feelings, but rocks must be solid. Similarly, Chaos can change and surge, but Order must follow its rules.

The concept of emotionally solid is that a man can have feelings and emotions, but they do not control his response. It's also the ability to endure the strong emotions of others, particularly his wife. He must remain a rock even in the mightiest storms.

To be emotionally solid is to remain calm through your wife's fiercest anger and most profound, darkest sadness. It is to suffer a loss and still be able to hold and comfort your wife and children. It is to share your feelings without surrendering your self-control to those feelings. Even if confronted by overwhelming feelings, you can hold onto yourself. Such a man can express dark emotions while maintaining a solid faith and confidence that God is greater.

To be emotionally solid is to be a foundation and source of strength for your wife, family, and community in even the worst circumstances—not through your strength alone but through your faith in the Lord. When you look at our greatest heroes, so many were effective not through their physical but their emotional strength.

Let's return to Christ. We know that Christ had powerful emotions. He was fully man as well as fully God. There are several situations where he shows and even shares these powerful emotions. The first one I want to consider is the story of the death of Lazarus, found in John 11.

Consider this story overall. When Christ cries (verses 35-36), it is so powerful that all around him are moved. Yet, knowing the strength of His sorrow, He made some interesting choices leading up to Lazarus's death. In verses 5-6, we find that even though Jesus loved Lazarus and his sisters, he chose to wait where he was for two days longer. Despite his strong emotions, his rock-like core was more robust. His central will did not lose control of His emotional urges.

After Lazarus has died, Jesus confronts his sisters and shows even greater strength. He shares his grief with these women but is always in submission to his purpose. I can imagine a desire to fix everything instantly. Nevertheless, He holds firm to the will of the Father.

Another example to consider is found in Matthew 26. Consider what happens when Jesus goes into the Garden of Gethsemane. He is so emotionally upset that he literally is sweating blood (a state I have yet to reach.) Despite this "weakness," He invites his closest friends to come with Him. He is strong enough to share Himself intimately with Peter, James, and John repeatedly through this dark hour.

Unhelped by these sleepy friends, Jesus's emotional strength continues to shine forth. At one point in prayer, He begs the Father to allow this cup to pass. He follows, however, with a statement of submission. He has these incredibly strong, powerful, and even dark emotions. Yet He never surrenders the control of His central will to them. His will remains united with the Father.

Such must we men aspire to become. We will never have the perfection that Christ offers, but I invite you to embrace the masculinity of emotional solidness. Here are a few practical steps:

- When you have big feelings, share them with your wife, family, and close friends, but only under the subjugation of your faith in the Lord. Maintain your response and hold onto your deeper truth. You must be the rock for your wife. She must be the waves, or all will go into disarray.

- If you cannot control your response to a feeling, if it is too dark or powerful, share it with another man you trust before you share it with your wife. You must honor the essence of who and what a man is. If your Order is failing, you must find another who can be Order for you. Your wife is not Order—nor do you want her to be. Find a faithful man you love, trust, and respect who will help you shoulder this burden. Share with him.

- When your wife or loved one has a big and powerful feeling, be the rock. A rock can listen, empathize, and even seek to understand. It is not emotionally volatile in response. Many practical tips to explore this issue will follow later.

- When the world seems to overwhelm you, return to your source. Return to the sacraments, particularly Confession and the Eucharist. Attend additional daily masses. Spend time in Adoration, offering these feelings and fears to the Lord directly. Seek to surrender to His will and trust in His goodness. Your rock must rest upon His foundation to withstand the storm.

CHRIST WAS NOT AFRAID TO USE HIS STRENGTH

Many men are genuinely afraid of their strength. There are several possible reasons for this. First, many of us were hurt by our own fathers' failure to control their strength. Many fathers were overwhelmed by the pressures of life and responded poorly. They established a tyrannical order rather than using their strength to protect and defend. This response can often be a desperate play for stability. I have seen myself do this when feeling overwhelmed. Do not, however, confuse the misuse of strength with the value of that strength.

Additionally, the powers of the world are afraid of male strength. The media, for instance, often highlights examples of men who have lost control. Rarely do we see positive examples of a powerful man conquering vice and wickedness. Do not be discouraged. If the devil did not fear the strength of men, he would not direct such attacks against it.

There are several Biblical examples of where Christ used strength. Let's explore a few. The first famous example is when Christ clears the temple, as described in John 2, starting in verse 13. There are several things we need to note about this passage:

- Christ is not using His strength for His benefit but for His Father's.

- Christ focused on the result, not hurting people (they could still talk to Him even after being driven out).

- The emotion present is often described not as "anger" but as "zeal." Sometimes, it is called "righteous anger" and is directed towards honoring the Lord. We must be careful; it is hard for us men to stay righteous while angry. We are selfish, prideful sinners who are eager and quick to disguise anger directed to our benefit as zeal.

Another example occurs in Matthew 23. Jesus powerfully denounces the Pharisees for their corruption. Although strong insults are almost a normal part of our daily lives in modern culture, this was not the case in the ancient world. What Jesus said would have been utterly shocking to all His listeners. Modern people might call this speech "offensive" or "hateful." Again, consider a few points about this story:

- Jesus focuses primarily on the immoral actions of the Pharisees, not upon themselves.

- Jesus seeks to protect the Jewish people first, not merely attack the Pharisees.

- His indictments focus on a call to reform. He invites them to improve.

- These statements occur after the Pharisees have been well warned by scripture and Christ Himself.

One final story comes from Luke 4. Jesus returns to Nazareth, testifies to the people there, and is utterly rejected. Then something interesting happens. They led him up to the cliff's edge, intending to hurl him off. There is a large crowd, including many powerful men. Somehow, despite all these, He "passed through the midst of them and went on his way."

Something powerful had to happen. It's not like Jesus escaped around the side and evaded their reach—He went right through the middle. Jesus is using great power, perhaps physical or His Divine will; we do not know.

Again, note some common elements. He did not use this power to serve primarily Himself. Being thrown off a cliff sounds far less painful than His Passion. Christ was the strongest, most capable man of all time. Yet, in all ways, He subjugates Himself to the Father. We must do likewise. We should expect the world to utterly reject us as well, but fear not, for Christ has conquered the world.

Do not be afraid of your strength. Nurture and develop it. Train yourself for combat, not only physically but also emotionally, intellectually, and, above all, spiritually. Then, when the Father directs you through discernment and prayer, gird your loins! Strive, fight, and struggle your way to victory. Do not fear your strength. Fear its misuse. We men can hurt our loved ones terribly by misusing our strength. Like any other skill, the better you understand it, the more likely you will use it well. If we use it correctly, we can heal generations of sin.

CHRIST GAVE UP EVERYTHING FOR OTHERS

You probably knew this one was coming. The crowning moment, the "hour" that Christ refers to throughout His ministry, is His Passion. Intellectually, you already know your life must include sacrifice. In our gut, however, we men often try to hide from this truth. It doesn't work. Here are some thoughts to consider:

- Do you surrender your comforts for the greater good of your family? If you drink too much or spend too much time engaged in leisure activities, will you surrender them to help your wife and children? They need you badly!

- Do you surrender your time to your family and community? In many ways, time is one of our most valuable and highly guarded assets. We often will be more generous with money than with time.

  Time is a great gift. Furthermore, do you give your attention entirely when giving your time? Are you deeply and powerfully present with your children? Do you attend to your wife and attempt to hear her heart through her myriad of drifting words? It is a struggle, but it is a worthy sacrifice!

- Do you surrender your physical body? You may need to find a more difficult job to support your family. Do you engage your children despite how tired you are? Do you show up and help your community? Whatever the details, are you willing to surrender your flesh?

- Do you surrender your sense of justice? What was done to Christ was wholly unjust in every way. Yet, He surrendered this and endured the Passion anyway. Throughout your life, there will be many moments when you must endure injustice—the most painful may come from those you love most. Are you willing to surrender your sense of justice?

Order shines the brightest and does the most good when directed towards the good of another. The rock that protects and shelters the most people in the hardest circumstances will take the most severe beating. It is our masculine goal to become this. Women spend their bodies on children, nurturing, healing, and restoring. They draw others in towards themselves. We men have an outward focus; God calls us to surrender ourselves for the outward good of others.

This purpose and calling give meaning to our lives. Lean into that Order; do not be scared of it. The cost may be high, but the cost of inaction is ever higher. *"Every man dies. Not every man really lives."* Yes, that line is from Braveheart (not the most virtuous of movies), but it's true!

CHAPTER SIX
MEEKED MASCULINE STRENGTH

STRONG *VS* HARD

I've explored several aspects of masculinity, and I want to expand upon one before considering relationships. In my work, I find that the concept of good masculine strength needs to be better understood. Few men are successfully meeked. I encourage you to develop and apply these strengths to all areas of your life.

What is the difference between "hardness" and "strength." Many men confuse these and mistakenly believe that to be strong is to be unmoving. There are moments, yes, when a strong man must hold firm. There are also moments when he must use his strength to move a heavy weight and change something in the world.

The "rock" model starts to break down on this idea. A large piece of granite is indeed firm and endures harsh elements well. It can support weight and bear the load. However, it is worthless if a wild animal jumps out of the woods and attacks a nearby child. In this sense, it is not strong; it cannot react and be dynamic. Strong, in contrast to hard, gives capacity for motion.

To be human is to have both stillness and motion. Sometimes, we must stand firm, but sometimes, we must yield. Sometimes, we must push hard, or sometimes, we must pull towards ourselves. We must be meek before the Lord to determine which is correct.

Sometimes, hurt men will swear off part of their strength. Perhaps they were physically abused as a child and disavow all violence. Later, they are unwilling to defend an innocent. They build walls around their pain with strong gates to keep themselves "safe." When a family tragedy strikes, he cannot access the inner strength Jesus displayed to Lazarus's sisters.

If you are hurt and have found yourself locking your emotions away (or perhaps suppressing them), you must confront this pain. You cannot be a man of strength with this part of yourself tied up. Seek help, but carefully. It is tough to find good help these days. What you need depends on the nature of your wound. I do not have space here to explore all the various types of help, but a good starting point is some critical self-honesty. Is it related to abuse that occurred as a child? Therapy might be the solution. Is this failure to carry forth a discipline you can but simply won't do? A strong male accountability partner or coach might help. You may not even know—and that's OK. Try something, and get help now!

I once met a man who worked out daily in the gym but only used a few weight machines he enjoyed. Because he did the same motions daily, he grew connective tissue that limited his other motions. When his crisis came, he needed strength in a different motion, but his muscles were too tight. He was unable to help. Frustrated, he found a new gym to develop all his muscles.

So many men limit themselves. We may develop our intellectual or physical muscles, but we are locked up and bound emotionally or spiritually. To be strong, we must have a full range of motion and be able to apply our strength safely in any situation.

Do not confuse hardness with strength. You must be able to feel. You must be able to share those feelings with strength and intimacy. A powerful man is strong in all domains.

FAILURE TO BE MEEK

Next, we must consider what directs our strength. All too often, we have handed the reins of our horse to someone or something other than the Lord. Some common "idols" to which we surrender control of our strength include money, sex, power, influence, reputation, anger, justice, or any other earthly good.

When we surrender our control, something else gains power over our lives. Whether surrendered to God or false "idols," your hands are not on the wheel. The difference is that God's plan for us is always good and beneficial. The forces of the world have no such intentions.

One interpretation of how spirits interact with humans is that when we surrender control to them, they "have their way with us." The sexual implication is intentional. If a woman surrenders her body to an immoral and lustful man, bad things happen. We train our children to avoid strangers for this reason. We men must be more vigilant against surrendering ourselves to these spirits of the world. Their "use" and consumption of our goodness are very similar.

The devil knows well how to trick us. He offers us a compelling fake promise. We far too easily surrender some piece of our lives, often getting some worldly good in exchange. The final damage, however, is far more significant than we expected. Sometimes, it takes years to see the damage, but it can be devastating. The devil will not hesitate to have his way with us if we allow him.

Comfort and pleasure are often the enemies of holiness. They are not intrinsically evil but are often part of the lure the devil offers us. The Bible and the teachings of the Saints are full of exhortations to reject comfort and pleasure and pursue the Cross instead. We humans are easily misled. The Cross offers safety and purpose. Surrender your reins to God alone.

The final way we often fail to be properly meeked is when we drop the reins entirely. This strong historical tradition goes back to the Garden of Eden. While the serpent is tempting Eve, Adam is standing right there. God charged Adam to care for the garden and all the occupants, especially his wife! Yet, he does nothing; he fails to act while the devil attacks Eve. Eating the apple was not his first failure. Adam then blames both Eve and God for his failures.

Dropping the reins is just as bad as surrendering them to an idol. The devil wins whenever we do not pursue God's will. Surrender everything to Him. Give Him the reins of your strength daily, even every moment, if needed! As you mature and become wiser, you will realize that you are a terrible director of your strengths. Give them to God. St. Philip Neri supposedly prayed, "Lord, beware of this Philip, or he will betray you!" We should all pray the same.

I'll share a painful example from my past. After I graduated with my Ph.D., I believed that I was terrific. I went to work for Intel doing research, and found myself very successful. Solving complex problems has always been a strength of mine, and that looked to still be true. I was cocky, obnoxious, and even condescending to those who disagreed with me. I never even realized something was wrong until a senior engineer from a distant group asked me to stay after one meeting.

"Michael, you are the most abrasive person I've ever worked with," Justin said grimly.

I paused; this was not what I had expected at all.

"We're all here for the same purpose: trying to make this product work. When you speak, you sound like you really think everything is about you."

I started to grow a bit defensive, but he cut me off first.

"Look, you're smart and talented, but if you want to be successful, you must set aside your ego and work with everyone else. If you can't work together with us, I doubt you'll make it very long."

I'll never forget the look on Justin's face. I paused and put aside my ego; he was trying to help me. Although he didn't use this word, he correctly called me out for not being meek. He invited me to allow the bigger picture and the needs of the company to lead.

SURRENDERING CONTROL TO JESUS

Knowing that we must surrender control to Jesus is easy. Most of us intellectually know that. We give consent to the idea in our heads, at least. We say, "Oh yes, Jesus is in charge, for sure!" Yet, when the dark moments come, we often regain control and do things we know are wrong.

On the one hand, God knows this will happen. That's why He gave us Confession. On the other hand, we do ourselves an injustice when we pretend like we've surrendered. The challenge is to surrender not on an intellectual level but on an emotional or "gut" level.

In Matthew 16:24, Jesus says we must "deny ourselves and take up the cross." What does this mean? What part of myself am I supposed to deny? Should I pretend that I don't have a left arm? Instead, this is an invitation to oppose my internal and disordered will. To do this properly, we must first acknowledge the broken and disordered nature of our wills.

Again, I encourage you to pray the Litany of Humility, found in the appendix. Pray slowly and thoughtfully, watching what rises within you to oppose the statements. Most of us are far more prideful than we realize. This litany and many other church writings call us to a deeper humility. We must fully acknowledge how utterly hopeless we are at fixing things ourselves. Surrender is the only option.

Consider how even our language twists words related to pride. Is "ego" a good thing or bad? Is it OK to take "pride" in a job well done or a positive review from a boss? How important is self-esteem? What does that even mean to a Christian? How do we balance what we want with what God wants? What if they are good things? These questions have challenging answers.

Rather than try to wade through that impassable and deadly jungle, I invite you to simply surrender. No matter how good a "good" you believe you are pursuing, God's will and goods are better. Always are. Just surrender every piece of yourself to His will. It sucks and is often horribly painful. The only thing worse is to depend upon yourself.

It is a guarantee that if you surrender the "good" you want to God, He will give you a better good in exchange, not necessarily at the time of your choosing nor in the way you would like. His promises do not come on our timelines or agendas. They are, however, unfailing. Our promises fail regularly and rarely deliver the good we seek. Don't fight His direction; surrender to it, surrender your strength, and regularly hand control to the Lord.

The final image I want to offer you is that of a "living sacrifice." When the ancient Israelites killed a bull or sheep to offer a sacrifice, it was dead on the altar. It cannot walk away. In the New Testament, Christ is the ultimate sacrifice, and we offer ourselves as a living sacrifice to "complete what was lacking" (Col 1:24).

Normally, sacrifices on an altar are dead. We're still alive, however, which means we have the ability to get up off the altar. All too often, we note how painful it is to be a sacrifice and choose to stop following God's will. In this metaphor, provided by Fr. John Riccardo, you can imagine we have the power to disconnect from and step away from the cross whenever we wish. God's invitation is to repeatedly go back to it every time. Step back onto the altar and offer yourself completely to Him. Repeat as often as necessary. It hurts. Every. Single. Time.

CHAPTER SEVEN
FINDING YOUR PURPOSE

PURPOSE MATTERS

One significant difference between masculinity and femininity is the need for purpose. Chaos does not need a purpose or plan. The primal energy of Chaos can surge in any direction at any time. Ideally, it will flow along the paths laid out by Order. If the Order reshapes, Chaos will adapt.

Order, however, must have a purpose. Why are we redirecting the water in this direction? What will it accomplish? When an architect designs a bridge, there is a specific canyon he designed it to cross.

Without a purpose, there is no Order. Imagine going into IKEA and purchasing many different products that all require assembly. At home, instead of assembling them one at a time, you open all the boxes at once and assemble pieces randomly. It's hard to imagine that whatever monstrosity you create will be helpful. When a man has no purpose, his life will end up like this IKEA monstrosity: a bunch of randomly attached events that don't add up.

Neither money nor women can be your purpose. Men commonly overemphasize both. Money is merely a tool for your actual purpose. Your woman is the Chaos that will bring life and energy to your quest. You must have an intent for the water you steer with your rock.

PURPOSE AND GOD

Most of us intellectually know that God must be a higher priority than anything else—even our wives. We like to give intellectual assent to the idea that if we (somehow) had to make a choice, we would choose God. But the choice is rarely apparent— at least not enough for us to endure disappointing our wives.

While fear of disappointing a wife is virtually universal, it is often unavoidable and sometimes even necessary. There is a mess if a rock blocks the flow of waves to steer the water. The wave will smash hard into the rock and apply pressure to it. This pressure does not mean the rock is in error. It is not, however, comfortable.

When a man assumes a purpose in his life, there are times when that purpose must be a higher priority than the desires of his wife. If God has given you a purpose, it comes with His priority. If the purpose isn't from God, then what good is it? If your wife is unhappy because you need an evening to work on this purpose, you may have to endure her unhappiness. Wise men, however, confirm that decision through prayer.

This constraint is particularly common when you have little children. Little children are a heavy burden, period. They can be delightful and rewarding but remain a hefty burden. It is normal to both love them and be desperate for time away from their care. Your wife is reasonable not to want to continue caring for them after you get home!

One of the jobs of the masculine is to set the course for the family. Sometimes, this means working on a project after 5pm, leaving your wife to care for the children. I'll caution you not to overplay this card. If you need to engage in this plan, provide ample and abundant alternate times when your wife can be free from the children. Perhaps over the next 3-4 evenings, you can take the kids entirely and give her time off on Saturday morning. You'll need to discuss with her what she thinks would be helpful.

God's will is never for you to be cruel or a tyrant. If you prioritize any idol over your commitment to your wife and kids, she will resist your lead. By contrast, if you serve your family well, she will be more likely to trust your lead. Embracing God's purpose for your life should never be an excuse to punish a spouse.

To be a masculine man means two things that may seem conflicting:

1. You must serve your wife and children powerfully and frequently, surrendering your wants (but not legitimate needs) to the family's good.

2. You must also lead your family—sometimes even in a direction that they do not agree with or like. You are the leader. The responsibility and authority are yours unless you abandon them.

I strongly encourage you to share your beliefs and convictions with your wife—especially when they might conflict with her wishes. Listen to her desires and ask yourself if you can help meet them differently. (e.g., If you need Thursday evening, what extra can you do Wednesday and Friday to help?) Lead her in a way that makes her feel valued, appreciated, and needed. Communicate to her your love of the Lord and your desire to follow His will. Ask her to pray and listen to what she says. The Lord speaks differently to women, sometimes more than men. Leading is always your job, but you better listen carefully to your wife!

When my wife and I started our coaching businesses, they did not perform anywhere near as well as we expected. We were losing money, patience, and any sense of progress. Intellectually, we both thought the grand experiment had failed.

Despite our desire to give up, our prayers directed us to keep going. I believed God was telling me that my purpose would not be found in the corporate world. We both felt the call to try to help people who were hurting. While there continue to be many bumpy moments that don't quite work out, I still believe this is the path God wants us on. It has not been comfortable or easy, but I believe that the corporate world would have been worse for us.

IF YOU DO NOT FIND A PURPOSE, YOU WILL BE WEAK.

What is Order when there is no objective to the Order? Imagine your boss at work showing up one day and instructing you to create a new rule system for the company. You might reasonably ask, "What do you want these to accomplish that's different from how we operate now?" Imagine he responds that he wants nothing different—just new rules for change.

This request would likely be confusing and frustrating, but how you would even create it is unclear. How does one structure new rules when there's no desired change? Why change at all? The whole exercise seems destined to fail. The new rules would likely be worse than what you have now.

You will impose Order upon yourself and your surroundings. If this Order is not for some purpose, you are in trouble. Not only will you have difficulty persuading others to follow your plan, but you will also likely make things worse. Imagine going up to your wife and saying, "The whole family is going to all get up two hours earlier in the morning and go to bed two hours earlier. I have no purpose for this other than it's something we could do."

It would be painful and difficult to adjust the circadian rhythm of all the children—and to what end? She would likely resist; even if she complied, it would cause problems.

This sort of change would be very different if it had a purpose. My wife and I adjust the kids' wake-up times by an hour yearly to balance daylight. Summers here have very long days (16 hours of light), and we've found that our kids go to sleep more easily when it's dark. When winter comes, the light is gone by dinner. We prefer they get up earlier to align with our preferred homeschool schedule. The purpose of changing their bedtimes is to maximize the children's sleep and education. With such a powerful purpose, adjusting schedules makes sense, is compelling, and is valuable. It gives me the strength to insist upon it when my children complain.

Beware the man without a purpose. Consider a man who returns to his parents' basement without a medical need. He likely has no job, agenda, or purpose in life. He is the weakest version of himself. Women will not want to reproduce with him. Young men will not choose him as a mentor. Older men will only commit to helping him if he changes.

I love the outdoors. I have two very different outdoor camping trips: trips that involve chasing large animals while carrying a gun and trips that do not. The former has a clear and powerful purpose: a successful hunt. Therefore, I go to bed early, eat healthy, and get a ton of exercise. Every hunting trip makes me stronger and wiser. The latter is much more casual. I stay up late in discussions, drink a bit too much, and try to sleep in. Many excellent conversations have come from both types of trips. I enjoy them both, but I'm not confused about which is better for my health.

Unlike the minor weakness caused by a couple of days of camping, lacking a purpose for your life creates a profound weakness. It will permeate many different aspects of your life. Why get up early? Why do any of the basics? We men must have a solid "why" to thrive.

Find a powerful purpose. It will give you a powerful strength, draw others to you, and propel you toward holiness.

WOMEN ARE ATTRACTED TO A MAN PURSUING HIS PURPOSE.

Men and women all want to be attractive—this is universal. Some may have buried this desire out of fear, but the core desire is always there. Basic female attractiveness is comparatively simple. Men like curves. We also like softness—physical and emotional. Entire industries help women become more attractive.

What makes men attractive is more subtle. Let me make it simple: Strength. Strong men are attractive, period. Confidence is a result of strength. I don't mean merely physical strength (though that does help). Still, even more so, emotional, economic, intellectual, and spiritual strength are all incredibly attractive—both sexually to women and platonically in both men and women.

Individuals will value different strengths differently, but it all returns to strength. A large bank account is a type of strength, as is confidence. A powerful emotional presence indicates strength, as does the ability to captivate a room with musical skill. Strength is attractive.

Thus, if pursuing a purpose makes men strong, it also makes them attractive. Remember this as you plan your life. You want to work continually to attract your wife if you are married. If you are single, you want to attract a potential future wife. If you are at work, you want to attract attention from your boss and coworkers. If you are in a social situation, you want to get approval from others.

It feels good to be high in the hierarchy of male strength! If you are an expert cyclist, you enjoy being in an environment where cycling is valued. Whatever your strength, it's fun to live in it.

You need to have a powerful purpose you are pursuing to be strong. Without it, your confidence will weaken. Your ability to hold attention is greatly diminished. You probably don't even like yourself. Women do not want to marry a man who is content to live in his parents' basement.

While marriage and family provide some purpose, many marriages grow cold if the man does not have a greater purpose outside the home. Your wife is likely not aware of her diminished attraction. She may withdraw in small and subtle ways that weaken the marriage. You do not want this.

DON'T ACCEPT EXCUSES. DON'T BLAME.

We men are excellent at making excuses and blaming others. (Women are, too; they do it differently.) You see it in the very opening pages of the Bible. Right after God calls Adam to task about the apple, Adam doesn't hesitate to blame both Eve and God. "The woman whom You gave to be with me, she gave me fruit." (Italics added to emphasize the blaming.) What might have happened if Adam had accepted responsibility, apologized, and asked for forgiveness?

Don't do what Adam did. Yes, you have some unfortunate events in your past that will complicate your ability to pursue your purpose. Yes, things do go wrong. Too. Bad. An easy victory does not make you a man. Instead, a man struggles relentlessly against superior odds and rises repeatedly to throw himself into the battle. The greatest achievements made are in the most hopeless situations.

I had many traumatic experiences in childhood that provided me with excellent excuses for years. For most of the time, I wasn't even aware of them. I decided I shouldn't have to deal with more garbage, yet garbage came my way. My response was to snap, crack, and attack.

It wasn't until I realized my temper was my responsibility to solve that my life improved. When I realized that my wife and kids could do things I didn't like, but I didn't have to get mad, I was able to love them better. I am still discovering today the excuses I have allowed to continue.

You may have had terrible parents. You may have been abused as a child. You may not be the most intellectually or technically gifted. You may have married someone who now disappoints you. Perhaps through bad luck, you've had a significant financial setback. Too bad! Pursue your purpose anyway. Especially for situations occurring in adulthood, the odds are that you are far more to blame than you want to admit. Whether it is your fault or not, do not blame. Do not offer excuses. Get up, return to the Lord, and Do The Work.

DON'T GET LOST IN THE LITTLE TASKS. KEEP THE BIG PICTURE IN MIND.

Another common way to avoid our purpose is to be consumed by the little tasks. To be fair, little tasks matter! The details of life are often essential to work out. However, there is a vast difference between being dutifully attentive to the little details versus using those details as an excuse to avoid doing your more significant purpose.

Some little tasks may be unnecessary, e.g., social media or television. While they can be fun, you must prioritize accordingly. Sometimes, we justify extra tasks with a clever label. "I'm fixing all the bikes for the family!" Some tasks are essential but poorly timed. The question is, are they the right thing to be doing *right now?*

We know when we have something important to do. We also feel (and run from) the discomfort of our purpose. Are a few distractions a big deal?

The cost is far higher than we think. Let me use an example to illustrate. Imagine you are working to build a house for your family before winter. You start in the spring and have several months of warmth. A few early distractions surely cannot be a big deal. The problems begin when September has a cold spell. It's not yet cold enough to pose a danger, but cold fingers and moist wood slow the work down. As temperatures continue to drop, the work becomes increasingly difficult. Suddenly, you're in danger of not finishing in time, and your family will likely suffer. If the devil cannot lead you to sin, he will keep you busy.

God gives us a specific task to do at a particular time. He does not give us a long list of tasks to do later. God's will is always expressed in the "right now." This timing is because it would be overwhelming to handle more than that. If God gives us a task to do "right now, "He has a good reason for it to be "right now." Unfortunately, we rarely get to see that reason. Yes, there might be a bit of flex in the timing—but there might not be! You play roulette with far higher stakes than you realize.

I struggle with this problem frequently. One typical example of getting lost in the details is when I'm doing a house project. I'm not very good at them, and I hate to leave projects in a potentially hazardous state. It's common for me to stop attending to my wife and children and pursue the project exclusively. The result is often a (poorly) fixed house for a family that feels unloved. That's not right.

A man does what is right and does it at the right time. Thus, he becomes strong and dependable. It's part of what makes him a good rock. Do not allow little temptations to pull you away from your purpose.

REGULARLY RETURN TO PRAYER.

Our purpose can and will change. It may change slowly or overnight. Sometimes, God points us in a particular direction not because we're supposed to achieve that goal but because we need to move a bit down the road.

I once spoke to a man who had this happen. His family struggled financially, and he feared he could never afford a house. Suddenly, it looked like the stars aligned, and they were approved for a loan that matched a price drop on the perfect house. He was sure it was a sign from God to buy that house.

The family spent weeks cleaning, packing the rental, and organizing their various storage units to prepare everything for the big move. All the references and paperwork were approved, but the deal suddenly failed.

At first, this man was angry. His family had worked so hard; he prayed and discerned the will of the Lord. Why had He teased them so? Why was He playing with their hearts? For some time, it was a struggle to pray with gratitude.

Then, the curveball came. Another house, an even better fit for their family and a better deal, went on the market. The seller was motivated to move very fast—it was a requirement for the sale. My friend's family had everything ready; it was an easy contract to negotiate. He realized that if he hadn't spent all that time getting ready for the first house, he never would have been able to capture the second house. God had never intended the first house; He simply used it as a target to get them moving and ready.

When Abraham ascended Mount Moriah, he was unaware of God's plans. God told Abraham clearly what to do, but not why. Abraham's faith was sufficient to get him moving in obedience. If that was all Abraham did, the story may have ended in tragedy.

Abraham was ready (and likely eager) for a change in the plan. Despite what must have been heart-wrenching fear and perhaps anger, Abraham kept communication with God open. He listened for the plan to be updated.

So, too, must we be attentive to the Lord. We must pursue our purpose with dedication and commitment, but we must always be open to changing that plan and purpose. God's ways are always higher and better than ours. We do not get to know them. We only have faith that they are better. Trust in Him. Pray regularly with open ears and the potential to change. Keep asking the big questions, and listen to His answers in whatever form.

CHAPTER EIGHT
BUILDING POWERFUL RELATIONSHIPS

This chapter will focus on how to lean into your masculinity to improve all your relationships. Much of this will apply to your marriage, and I will develop it further in the next chapter. For now, be confident that becoming what God intended you to be will improve all of your good and holy relationships.

HOLD POWERFULLY TO THE TRUTH AND THE FAITH.

The first and most crucial aspect of relationships is never to compromise yourself. Particularly as a representative of Order, you cannot be contradictory. Your Order crumbles into Chaos when you compromise. A Rock cannot stand for two opposite things at once. It becomes a noodle.

What issues are important to stand firm upon? Changing your preference for food or entertainment does not compromise who you are. It's essential to always be honest (or at least not lie—and that is something different), but these things do not become part of your identity.

Imagine, for a moment, an inner self that looks like a little man who lives inside you. When you act with integrity and honor, he stands tall, and his shoulders are back. When you are dishonorable, evasive, or do not do what you know is right, he cringes and gets smaller. This little man is not only a reliable image of yourself; he indicates your strength and ability to stand firm in the world.

A man does not have to wonder if he is guilty of lust when he ends up in another woman's bed. Similarly, he also does not have to wonder if he has lost integrity through his words and actions. We feel the truth through our bodies. We feel weaker and smaller. You undoubtedly have felt this in the past. It is not an enjoyable feeling. The consequences are far higher than the feeling suggests.

Your most important truth to cling to is that of your faith. Faith is the ultimate rock upon which your rock must be based. If your faith is compromised, you are indeed in trouble. If you compromise in a grave way, go to confession. Even if it is not a serious matter, repent in prayer before the Lord. Commit to doing better next time. The Lord will forgive and will heal, but you must repent and seek His healing. As a man, this foundation is just so much more important than most of us want to think.

DO NOT CHASE AN INNER RING.

You will inevitably encounter highly selective groups. They may occur in school, at work, in your parish, or wherever people gather. There are always some who want to form an exclusive group that, from the outside at least, looks very attractive to be part of.

C. S. Lewis calls these groups "inner rings" and writes about how toxic they are to pursue. Not only do they rarely deliver what appears to be promised from the outside, but even more importantly, they often require an individual to compromise himself to gain admittance. Even once you are finally "in" the exclusive circle, you will likely find only disappointment and soon begin seeking a different, better "inner ring."

It is a powerful attraction to our human pride and fallen nature to be part of a group that is somehow "better." This concept appears across all religions and cultures. Like most attractions to our pride, the damage done by pursuing such a group is subtle and layered. The voice in our head might say, "Well, just do it this once, and I'm in!" or "It can't really be that bad if everyone else has done it, right?" These need not at all be sexual and can regard any aspect of sin or compromise.

Only one type of "inner ring" is truly worth having. That is the inner ring of actual competence. If you become a doctor, work and strive to become the best doctor you can be. Without intending it, you will realize that you have become part of an inner ring of competent and hard-working doctors. Other competent doctors will recognize your efforts and treat you slightly differently—not maliciously, but because you are deemed trustworthy.

This particular inner ring takes hard work, sacrifice, and virtue to join. You likely will only realize it exists after you have joined it. Whatever your profession or vocation, others attempt to pursue the work with honor and integrity. Over time, they will recognize you, and you will recognize them. Like many virtue-related goods, this recognition comes from pursuing virtue itself.

I fell into this trap when I first started working in corporate life. There was a group that postured and fought over appearances. To gain their approval, you were required to work extra-long hours and be extremely connected to the job at all hours. Many of them would regularly wake up multiple times at night to check machine status and respond to emails. Many of them were single; some had negative views about children.

After a few months of trying to earn the approval of this group, I realized my relationship with my wife was suffering.

She dutifully allowed me to immerse my time into the job under the general appeal of "this is what my job needs me to do." I decided to stop this pursuit and pay the cost in popularity.

A few years later, however, I realized more about how corporate decisions were made. Those willing to spend all their time on the job indeed got promoted more quickly and were louder in meetings.

Still, there was a second round of discussions that happened very quietly. It was a discussion that occurred between two people in a cubicle. Each group had a few engineers who knew how to get things done efficiently—and we all learned how to identify each other. The decisions made in these meetings were often presented to the "hard workers" without their realization.

When I just tried to do my job well while also loving my family well, I earned my way into this more quiet group. It wasn't as glamorous, but it was often even more effective. Better yet, I had the family connections that really mattered.

DON'T CHANGE YOUR MIND TO PLEASE OTHER PEOPLE—ONLY DO IT BECAUSE IT'S TRUE.

At first, this one may sound like it will cost you friends and relationships. Indeed, it will, but only for those not worthy of your time.

We have all met men whose opinions change with the wind. While not a virtuous trait for either gender, it is particularly troubling for men who want to have a strong masculinity. A rock cannot change directions whimsically. Masculinity must be solid.

Of course, there will be times when others persuade you (likely over time) that a different perspective is actually true.

I have forgiveness and understanding for politicians who hold different views now than when they were youths, provided they can explain and justify their views now and apologize if necessary for their earlier views. I have little respect for a politician whose views change from audience to audience.

There is nothing wrong with careful consideration if confronted with a barrage of evidence for a differing opinion. In this consideration, you may discover that you don't truly care. That's ok. Honestly, most opinions in this world don't matter. They change often and have little to no impact. What's more important is that you be true to your word.

There are a lot of responses that a man can give without violating his masculinity. Some great examples include:

"I don't consider this issue important enough to me to be worth the time it would take to think it through."

"I suspect you may be partly right, but this won't affect my life right now, and I want to focus on other things."

"I disagree, but do not have the time to pursue it."

"I disagree, and your arguments do not persuade me, but I want to talk about other things."

For many (myself included), holding our opinions is too easy. However, standing firm is more difficult for those more inclined towards people-pleasing. Whatever your challenges, you must live in integrity.

I've worked with several men who really struggled with saying "yes" too much. Here's an example story that comes up with almost every one of them.

Fred, wanting to be a better husband, commits to a date night with his wife every Wednesday.

Every other night of the week had some sort of activity, but they had cleared Wednesdays. His wife found a babysitter to care for the children. For the first time in years, everything seemed to be perfect.

Wednesday arrives; around lunchtime, Fred's boss walks into his cube. "Fred, I need you to take over a critical task force. They meet every Wednesday night, and you need to be there."

Fred squirms in his seat. He knows the right thing to say but is afraid to say it. Hanging his head, he replies, "Sure thing, boss, I'll take care of it!"

Fred is terrified to tell his wife. He knows how much this date night means to her. Instead, he waits until the last minute and texts his wife: "Honey, there's an issue at work. I'm probably going to be 10 minutes late!"

An hour later, Fred finally leaves work. Walking into the front door, Fred tries to apologize profusely. His wife does her best to support him and looks forward to next Wednesday.

Unfortunately, Fred still doesn't have the guts to tell his wife what he committed to. The following several Wednesdays go down similarly. He still hasn't owned what's going on.

All his wife knows is that she doesn't feel loved, seen, or prioritized.

We all know where this story goes next. As a man, you often see what you need to do. Do it, even if it makes others unhappy. If you truly don't know, start praying right now. Don't be a wimp—it costs too much!

BE BOLD. LOVE DEEPLY. GIVE FULLY.

The devil often tempts men to do something "partly." When Peter asked Jesus how often we should forgive our brother, even Peter offered seven times. To a Jew of the time who is familiar with "an eye for an eye and tooth for a tooth," this likely sounded very generous indeed! Instead, our Lord responds with a much deeper "seven times seventy," indicating unending forgiveness.

Consider the depth of Christ's sacrifice and suffering through His Passion. Many theologians speculate that Christ suffered much more than necessary to achieve forgiveness. Even if His death was required, what Christ endured was far beyond that. If you have never watched Mel Gibson's The Passion movie, I encourage you to do it sometime. It helps to see a piece of what Christ went through out of love for us.

Father John Riccardo expands on this note to the idea that Christ suffered so much so we don't feel alone. No matter how much we suffer, we never outdo Him. We know He is there with us in any suffering we encounter. Even through the most horrible suffering, Christ loved us.

Christ was fully committed to the Father. Similarly, he invites us to engage deeply and fully with Him. In Revelation 3:16, Christ says that the lukewarm will be spit out of His mouth. It's a strong warning that modern comfort-focused people should take seriously.

In a similar way, Christ calls us to love others deeply. We are often luke-warm in all our relationships, choosing comfort over risk.

God did not create you to be lukewarm. Deep love is terrifying. It opens the possibility of profound rejection. Yet, shallow love should still be scarier, as it destroys the possibility of real connection and intimacy. There is no real possibility of gain without the risk of loss.

You may be in a relationship that doesn't seem fair to love deeply. Perhaps your wife has hurt you repeatedly over the years. Perhaps your father has been disrespectful to you since you left the house.

Whatever the details, I understand you might believe others don't deserve deep and full love. You are right! They don't "deserve" it—and neither do you.

We do not give love because the other person has earned it. That is not the model of Christ. All have sinned and fall short of the glory of God, yet God loves us more than we can imagine. We can never earn God's love. He gives it freely and asks us to do the same.

If you have children, you are called to be an earthly image of The Father to them. Love them without reservation! If you are married, you are called to love your wife as Christ loved the Church (this means crucifixion and the Passion).

The second greatest commandment is to love your neighbor as yourself. There is no person whom you are called to love slightly.

If you want a full and powerful relationship:

1. Do not hold your inner self back.

2. Give fully and deeply.

3. Selfless love is the only competition allowed.

4. Give of yourself, knowing that they will take advantage of you. Christ did no less.

DO NOT FAKE COMMITMENT.

Many have probably heard, "Fake it till you make it." This approach does work for some things—especially for men. Chaos must be in the moment and surging naturally. Order, by contrast, seeks to impose a constraint upon a system that initially may not feel natural. That's okay, as long as you fake the action (not the commitment).

Many people think that feelings come from the actions around us. Sometimes, yes, this is true. I told you the story about our tire-chasing puppy. After it died, we performed an impromptu funeral, and we all cried as we prayed. What's funny is what happened next. We headed back inside, and my wife and I attempted to plan something different. Despite the kids' protests that it would not be fun, we loaded everyone into swimsuits and headed to the beach. After ten minutes of playing with their friends, the kids laughed again. How did this occur?

In a natural way, feelings follow actions also. Test this sometimes; if you are feeling down or upset, try doing the actions you would if you were happier. Even something as simple as smiling can profoundly impact your emotions. You will soon find yourself feeling happier.

There are many times in life when we men must take action contrary to our feelings to bring about the Order we seek. It can often help to "fake" those feelings while performing the actions. The feelings usually become "real" as we do it!

Men cannot fake commitment. A man must be either committed or not. Commitment (like love) is not a feeling but a choice. If you claim a false commitment, the other person will figure it out, even if only subconsciously. Not only does this undermine your leadership (who wants to follow a lie?), but it also undercuts your effectiveness. If you are not fully committed, then your brain and body will not perform the same actions.

I enjoy hunting and have practiced with both bows and rifles. I've also trained many children to shoot. There's something funny I've watched play out many times. If someone hesitates about shooting a target, they usually find a way to miss it. If someone decides to hit it, they are much more likely to do so.

For example, one of my children genuinely feels sad for a deer when she sees it in the scope during hunting season. Many deer have escaped from her cross-hairs, even with an easy shot. She didn't want to shoot the deer; her body did the rest.

This concept is true for every aim we have in life: commit fully or change targets. There can be no middle ground.
You don't need to promise to achieve your aim; you may still miss it. Putting everything you have into a struggle and still failing is not failure; it is learning and growth. Failing to embrace the battle entirely invites a more profound failure, a failure of your will. This failure lingers and spreads.

Go through your life and the commitments you've made. Yes, the commitment to children's soccer is less than the commitment to attend Mass. You're allowed to have a hierarchy of priorities. You will know when you've faked a commitment because you will feel hollow when you pursue it. You will know you're holding yourself back.

If you doubt whether you should commit to something, don't. This action may disappoint others—that's ok! Better disappointment now than a much deeper failure later. If you review your life and discover that you have made commitments you shouldn't have, then unmake them quickly. Apologize for your error and announce your new intentions clearly. Do not leave gray space for yourself to procrastinate.

Waves are allowed to change directions at a whim. Rocks must be stable and firm. Be a man who honors his commitments and chooses them carefully.

PUSH YOURSELF AND YOUR FRIENDS TO THE EDGE—AND A BIT BEYOND.

Teenage boys often push each other to attempt risky and even dangerous actions. Whether cliff jumping, skiing over jumps, dirt biking, skateboarding, or other extreme physical actions, the boys keep pushing each other with taunts to try something even harder. They enjoy the push, and even when they fail, they seem satisfied.

The girls watching do not understand why the boys do this, but they eagerly await the results! The boy who pushes the hardest and wins gets the most female attention. Why would the girls be drawn to someone who seems crazy?

Now, I'm not encouraging you to go out and engage in high-risk behavior like a teenage boy. The odds are that your body is nowhere near as resilient as it used to be. I claim there are still other pushes left from which you will benefit. Push (or challenge) is essential to masculine identity and development.

Let me try to explain with an image. If your masculinity represents Order, then its job is to carve a bit of controlled space out of Chaos. Imagine our hero, St. George, slaying a wild bull. He carves out a bit of Chaos and tames it. He gains the food and resources from that brave action. Soon, however, he becomes bored; these woods are tame. Furthermore, he's used up whatever resources he found here. It's time to expand.

Our hero carves an even bigger chunk of Chaos as he slays a small dragon. He finds more gold, treasure, and food as he does this. Throughout his life, this masculine hero must increasingly claim and tame Chaos.

Now, let's introduce another element. Here is Evelyn; she is looking for a husband. George conquered one acre of Chaos, while Henry conquered two. Evelyn knows (at least on a subconscious level) that two acres will contain more resources for her and potential future children. Henry becomes more attractive as a partner. Women are attracted to strength and achievement.

Now, add even more people to the equation. Both George and Henry are friends. They both want each other to succeed and find a wife. However, thousands of men compete for the best women in this region. George and Henry are doing each other a favor by pushing each other to carve out bigger and bigger pieces of Chaos. They know this will mutually increase their attraction to women—and their chances of finding the right one. It's a favor to each other!

POWERFUL CATHOLIC MASCULINITY

In this much larger population, some men will be incredibly successful at conquering Chaos. Henry and George cannot settle for mediocrity! It makes sense for them to risk pushing each other a bit beyond their limits. First, they'll often discover that their limits are further than expected. Furthermore, if they are good friends and one goes too far, the other can help keep him safe. That little bit of extra push is required to really find (and develop!) your potential as a man.

You may not have a male friend who pushes you; if not, go and find one! Even if you cannot, you can push yourself. Being pushed is a primal need for a man to remain strong and masculine. If you lack a friend for safety, you must be more gentle with your limits, but you cannot relax!

It is all too easy for men to fall into comfort and complacency. If we do, we might discover that because our wives start complaining about it. The problem is that they do not know how to push us effectively and helpfully. The language gap is too large, and each side misinterprets the other. Your wife is not intended to be your push, but she likely will attempt to fill in the gap if you stagnate. At best, this is her operating in her masculine energy, which will kill off attraction. At worst, it leads to emotional discord and separation. You need another man.

CALL FORTH THE GOODNESS IN OTHERS.

In the story of creation in Genesis, God repeatedly "says" for things to be created. Each time He speaks, amazing things come to be. This passage shows God's power of creation, which is brilliantly demonstrated daily in our lives. We, however, are made in God's image and likeness. My claim to you is that we have some (though different) creative power in our words as well—particularly as men.

When Order carves out a piece of Chaos, it aims towards a particular desire. If I cut down a forest, I might create a farm or a safe place for livestock. My stated purpose determines what that piece of Chaos becomes. This process is not limited to inanimate objects.

Your words can create change, especially for those you have authority over (your wife and children, most notably). If you call your children weak and lazy, they will become slightly more so. If you describe them as brave and strong, they will become braver and stronger. Psychology has explored this at great length, there are training guidelines for teachers emphasizing the power of calling out the good in children.

We men rarely consider the creative power of our words. Seeking to remedy a wrong, we point it out (often repeatedly). Indeed, this is sometimes necessary, but it must be weighed against the damaging side effects. When you speak words describing a person to that person, you are not merely acting as a scientific observer. You act as an authority with "creative" power to effect change through your words. It is imperative to balance negative feedback with positive affirmations.

An authoritative source can cause an attribute to grow even if it is limited initially. Let's imagine a young boy who struggles to share his toys. There likely will be some improvement by simply yelling at him each time, but there is a lot of collateral damage. If you describe him as "a sharing boy," he will likely improve. If you catch and compliment his acts of sharing, he'll improve even more.

When our children were born, I was invited to call the girls "sweet girl" to encourage them to become sweeter. It's become so commonplace that they no longer even notice it. Of course, they are not always sweet, kind, and gentle, but why not tilt the odds in our favor?

When Jesus founded His Church, it contained the seeds for radical ideas that would forever change our world. Before the rise of Christendom, the concepts "each human has an inherent dignity and worth" or "all people have a likeness to the divine" were utterly unknown. These ideas transformed our society; they support every level of our legal and justice system. We must invite them into our own lives as well.

When speaking to another person, remember that you are exercising part of your divine likeness, which may have a far more creative effect than expected. Rather than "describe the good" in another person, I invite you to "call forth the good." You have probably read or watched the story of some hero who succeeded because someone "believed in" them. Every person you encounter, you have the power to push towards the heroic or failure. Choose your words well.

ENJOY BOTH YOUR FRIEND'S CRITICISM AND COMPLIMENTS.

There is great value in being challenged by your friends. I want to go further and invite you to consider "criticism" from another man as a blessing. Indeed, there are times when another man may attack you out of malice or spite—there is no need to enjoy or seek those out. It's common, however, that one man's words to another might sound vicious (especially to women) but be a subtle form of compliment.

A well-meaning man who criticizes you is doing two things at once:

- First, he is challenging you to grow. The masculine needs a push.

- Second, he indicates that he believes you are strong enough to withstand this attack. You are solid enough not to crumple.

Recognize that when a masculine man doesn't engage in this playful criticism, that is the negative critique. He considers you too weak to absorb the blow, so he refrains out of consideration for your overall health and welfare. This evaluation is not good— he has a low opinion of you. He will not trust you to stand by his side when the storm comes.

Masculine-style banter is extremely rare among women. I strongly encourage you not to engage with your wife or other women. It is not generally helpful. Feminized men may also view male banter in a negative light. If you fear this banter, consider which of the two following reasons might be at play:

- Possibly you genuinely are too weak to handle the banter

- You might be strong enough, but merely misunderstand the purpose

It is time to toughen up if you fall into the first category. If you have severe childhood trauma holding you back, head to a therapist. If you simply need a kick in the butt, look for a coach or mentor. I have helped many men grow in strength through my online programs.

If you fall into the second category, your path is more straightforward. It's time to start rewiring. Go on a men's retreat, ideally something rugged in the woods or other difficult terrain. As you struggle and work beside other men, you'll observe this banter start to take place. Watch closely how the men who are confident in their masculinity respond. They generally begin by smiling and then return the favor with their own banter. Both men will likely be laughing shortly. These are not attacks but bonding.

It is only from a man willing to criticize you that you can fully enjoy a compliment. At first, it might seem like we all enjoy compliments. They feel good and sound great... but are they real?

You have probably experienced the pain of a false and fake compliment when later reversed (often embarrassingly).

Do not trust the compliments of a man who will not engage in banter and criticism (at least once he gets to know you). He may be people-pleasing, coming from weakness, or perhaps even manipulative. Find men who are strong in their masculinity. When, after much banter, a compliment does land, it will feel amazing.

From a strong masculine man, both criticisms and compliments can be a positive and helpful experience. The criticisms may hurt; for example, when they call us to an action we know we are avoiding. Even those situations lead to more positive feelings when we finally do what we know we were avoiding.

A weak man will either not criticize you (causing concern about the genuineness of his compliments) or will sometimes criticize you from a place of malice. Do not regard his feedback. Invite him to grow in strength if possible and appropriate, though this typically requires an invitation. One example of an invitation is when you picked up this book—you invited me to challenge you to grow in your strength (wherever you are in your journey). Give the same value to other men in a spirit of charity and kindness.

YOU NEED STRONG AND FAITHFUL MEN IN YOUR LIFE.

Women are clear about their need for other women. They naturally join other women and share all the thoughts, feelings, and ideas going through their heads. If you are married, you must support your wife's need for other women!

Men, however, think we can make our way alone. Too many men struggle and fall without the support of their brothers.

We need the support of men just as much as women need other women!

Proverbs 27:17 is an often-quoted verse; you likely know it: "As iron sharpens iron, so one man sharpens another." Have you ever stopped to consider what iron sharpening iron must be like? The process produces friction, sparks, and a great deal of heat. Each piece of iron must be uncomfortable.

Throughout this chapter, I've repeatedly called you to find men to help you on your journey. I will end the chapter with a clear call to find those men. You cannot do this alone; even St. Anthony of the Desert started in a community. Cain asks of God, "Am I my brother's keeper?" Modern man must answer "yes" or face the fate of Cain.

Finding a good and faithful man willing to share your journey requires risk. You must be vulnerable and attempt to start a real conversation. You must ask them for help directly. Start with your parish or your extended family. Choose a man you respect and ask if he would be willing to meet you for coffee sometime to help you. If he says "no" or rejects your intimacy, keep looking!

If you cannot find a faithful and trustworthy man in your community, look beyond it. We live in a digital age, and help is available anywhere with an internet connection. As you explore online, you are looking for a man who will challenge you and is willing to make you feel uncomfortable. Such a man, whether coach, mentor, or guide, is one of the best investments you can make. Keep looking until you find one that fits and can help you!

Last, do not accept excuses. If you do not have any money, look for an older man who will help you for free. My first mentors were all unpaid. If you have little time, find someone very efficient and flexible. If your wife disapproves, then read the next chapter. Sometimes, good leadership isn't approved of.

At each stage of my life, a man has been ready to mentor and help me. God provides if we are willing to look. I've been mentored while working at Knights of Columbus events, skiing, coffee shops, office spaces, parish halls, and parties. If I wasn't open and willing to grow (often painfully) in my awareness of my shortcomings, it didn't work. Pray for a mentor and be willing to listen carefully.

CHAPTER NINE
PRACTICAL STEPS FOR HUSBANDING WIVES

In this chapter, I will use the terms "feminine" and "women" interchangeably. The reason why is that I am assuming that within your marriage, you want your wife to be in her feminine energy. Not only does this increase attraction, but it also brings balance and wholeness to your household. There are, of course, times when she must operate in a masculine framework, even at home. Many of the chores, disciplines, and confrontations that come up require a masculine response. Please understand that, for this chapter, I am focusing on when she is in her feminine.

TALKING AND WORDS

Research shows that, on average, women enjoy talking ten times more than men. Enjoy. Talking is pleasurable for us, but it is *ten times more enjoyable* for them. Imagine something you find great pleasure in doing—if there were no constraints, you also would spend a lot of time doing that activity. You might even keep doing it to the frustration and confusion of those around you!

Understand that the experience of talking, like the experience of shopping for purses or shoes, is something that women enjoy more than men, and they will likely want to do it a great deal more. What's perhaps different about talking is that it isn't an obvious difference at first. Have you ever been to a spot where you're kind of "talked out," yet your spouse still seems eager to go another few thousand words? It's easy to feel grumpy or perhaps even "used" in this situation.

The Church Fathers, and especially Saint John Paul the Great (JP2), write about the importance of a man not "using" his wife sexually. JP2 wrote that men can commit adultery in the heart, even with their wives. While this is a more grave form of "use" within a marriage, it is not the only type. What is the difference between "giving yourself to" and "being used by" another person? In marriage, these often seem hard to separate.

One difference between the two must be the intent of both parties. Suppose a wife willingly gives herself to her husband, and a husband willingly accepts the gift as a gift (not his due). In that case, a powerful act of love has likely happened. If the wife is deeply opposed to the union or the husband is unwilling to accept her as a gift, things start to go wrong. Pope JP2 further clarified that this difficult-to-understand teaching essentially appealed to human dignity. We must, as Christians, always respect the dignity of others.

How does this apply to talking? We men must stay aware of when we are in danger of letting ourselves be used. It's easy to allow our wives to drone in the background while our minds explore our current hobby. It's also easy to speak poorly in our thoughts about our wives while they "prattle" on. Communication requires the full attention of both parties to be successful. We give our wives a gift when we listen to them and pay attention to their words.

It's possible, however, to give this gift with resentment. When bitterness and resentment grow inside a heart, goodness withers. Your wife wants you to think highly of her, to desire her, and to pursue her. It makes her feel loved. Bitterness poisons this good. Consider again the example of sex. One of you desires sex more often than the other (usually the husband, but not always). The other will regularly have to decide if sex is a proper gift that can be freely given. If not, if bitterness about sex grows in the heart, the marriage suffers.

Have an open conversation with your wife. With great humility, bring up any areas in your marriage where bitterness is growing. If you're bitter about your conversations, try to make your request more specific. Explain your goal to have a deeper and fuller connection with her. Apologize for allowing the bitterness, and help your wife understand what you want and need. Commit to honesty going forward.

Sometimes, a spouse is called to give even if they don't want to, but they must still give freely. Sometimes, a spouse is called to say "no" when they cannot give freely. Be honest about when you simply cannot give her your focus and attention for a conversation, and be honest with yourself if you can but don't want to. You may be called to carry your cross a bit.

Note, I strongly recommend against describing "talking to your wife" as a "cross" where she might hear. While you must use tact, this is a critical issue to discuss. Being more transparent and honest can lead to powerful and intimate conversations.

While working with men, I've encountered many imperfect solutions to these struggles. For virtually any activity, one spouse will have a higher desire for that activity than the other. One of you wants to visit the in-laws more than the other. One of you wants to have dinner at home rather than go out to eat more than the other. This difference in desire intensity is not a problem.

The challenge is how the lower desire partner responds. Consider the times when your wife declines to have sex. Unless she handles it carefully, a rejection has the potential to feel like a blow. This danger is similar to any activity where the lower desire partner must gracefully decline a proposal from the higher desire partner.

Thankfully, a desire for talking is much easier to meet than a desire for sex. Your wife needs female friends. Her female friends share her love of talking and will gladly engage in that activity with her, helping meet her needs. Men need men, and women need women. Meeting this need is not optional if you want a happy marriage.

Be open with your wife about your needs and desires, whether about talking or any other activity. Identify which of you is the lower-desire partner and which is the higher-desire. Approach this discussion from the perspective: not only is this normal, but it's unavoidable to have one person want something more than the other. Likely, there are many interests you desire more than your wife. One example in my marriage is the desire to go hunting.

Women sometimes mistakenly believe that because their female friends love talking, men should also. It's easy for them to misinterpret your lower desire for words as a rejection of them. Emphasize this is not the case; you love her greatly! You are trying to love her better. It is much better to be genuinely attentive and present with her for 2000 words than to be distracted and mentally absent for 4000 words.

Give of yourself in a healthy way. Do not let yourself be used—it often leaves the man feeling bitter and the woman feeling rejected.

WOMEN ARE NOT HABITUAL LIARS (IN GENERAL).

When a wave surges to one side, then a few moments later surges back—is this an indication of intent to deceive?

"You told me you were a westward-traveling wave, and now you're going east!" A wise rock knows that waves are fickle and surge in all directions as the currents take them. Similarly, Chaos is surging and unpredictable (or else it would be Order.)

Women commonly use words in ways that confuse men. They exaggerate, often even say things that sound factually wrong, as their feelings surge. These words describe their feelings, not the physical world. This feminine behavior does not carry the same meaning as it would if a man were doing it. When the waves are surging in a woman's femininity, the words coming out are far more about the water currents than the rocks.

This confusion can upset a man, especially if he is sensitive to the truth. It can quickly feel like your wife is lying—habitually. Unfortunately, your desire for her to be consistent is effectively asking your wife to be more masculine, which can reduce attraction between the two of you. It's all too common for men to rant and rave over their wives' surging feelings and words without realizing that this is part of what makes them great.

Now, a clarification is needed. There are at least two modes of talking in the marriage. One mode is actual problem-solving. In this mode, the wife must assume a more masculine stance and partner with her husband to solve the problem constructively. While it may be difficult for her (and it is reasonable to expect her to switch to the other mode periodically), progress is limited unless she can hold a more practical conversation in this mode.

A second mode of speaking within a marriage is sharing feelings and emotions. This mode is very different and has very different objectives. In this mode, the goal is not to solve the problem but to connect emotionally. In this mode, a wife should slide into a more feminine perspective. She can gush and surge about all her feelings and perspectives.

Rather than view this as an attack (though the words would suggest such), a wise husband simply views this as the waves smashing back and forth.

In this mode, husbands should listen to their wives. Reflect on what they say, and attempt to understand and empathize with them as best they can. Understand you will likely never do this as well as her female friends—how could you? They speak her language naturally, while you are a foreigner. As you become better at this skill, it may surprise you to realize that men sometimes need to speak in this mode, too.

The problem is not that there are different modes but rather confusion when both parties do not understand the current mode! Even worse, sometimes, one person will switch back and forth between modes quickly. The other party (typically the husband) can struggle to keep up and is easily confused about how to respond.

When women speak with women, they can switch modes quickly, and the other women (generally) keep up with the current mode. They perhaps think that because their female conversations can work this way, conversation with their spouses should, too! By contrast, men tend to avoid the emotional connection mode except in the most intimate and sensitive times and places. Entering that mode is reserved for the closest friends only, in a very isolated moment, and marked by intense and specific words (or grunts.) Once two men enter the second mode, they cannot leave it without mutual agreement.

It's easy to see why communication in marriage is so hard. The basic assumptions going into a conversation are radically different. When I was first married, for example, my wife and I quickly realized we had radically different ideas about what Saturdays were for. In my family, Saturdays were a work-on-the-house day. We got up early (6 or 7) and started working right after a prompt breakfast. In my wife's family, coffee started around 9 or 10. They would spend the morning hours relaxing and conversing. After a slow and leisurely lunch, a few casual activities might be proposed. Our first Saturday together was a small bomb of realization of different expectations.

Thankfully, this particular Saturday, we laughed at the differences because we each rapidly realized that the root problem was simply different expectations. You can make much progress in your marriage conversation with similar realizations. The key is to help manage expectations by clearly communicating upfront. Each Friday evening, my wife and I learned to negotiate what the next day would look like.

Plan a conversation with your wife to discuss these different modes of communication and the importance of expectations. Explain to her what your expectations have been in the past and how you have related to others. Invite her to share her experiences and expectations. Discuss what it might look like for her to help you identify which mode she is in. I know many successful marriage partners who start every heavy conversation with the question, "Do you want to help fix this, or simply for me to listen?"

A fantastic surprise benefit of this question is that it encourages your wife to determine what she wants out of the conversation. It's common that she doesn't know. As the conversation progresses, if you suspect she has switched modes, lovingly ask her: "Honey, it seems like rather than wanting to express yourself, you seem to be asking for help to solve the issue. Is that right?" She may not even realize she has switched modes.

This process will require training and practice for both of you. You likely have radically different expectations about these types of communication, which may make you feel uncomfortable or even dislike it. Clear communication about expectations is essential because of the potential damage lurking behind a confused intent. It's easy to badly hurt feelings and damage charity if you are not on the same page.

One final note: women, like men, do sometimes legitimately lie. It could be out of fear, desire, or other human emotions. One of the benefits of clearing up this expectation is that it separates the many times a woman speaks her feelings with the potential of her husband feeling lied to from the times she actually does fall and legitimately intends to deceive. In the second mode above, she is not intending to deceive. Be humble when you hit these bumps: either party can always say, "I feel hurt by what you just said; please help me understand what you meant." Give them the benefit of the doubt. It will pay out more in the long run.

DON'T OVER-ANALYZE YOUR WOMAN'S WORDS.

The waves flow, the Chaos surges, and your wife uses words. It might be confusing or even feel threatening, but that's partly "working as intended." When women start talking negatively, many husbands feel intimidated and try to retreat. Many husbands do not know how to deal with strong negative emotions from their wife. They sound decisive and definitive (as if a man were speaking them), causing him to worry about the future of the marriage.

Instead, consider her words to be a snapshot of her feelings. Allow her to have big feelings. Part of her femininity will be suppressed if it cannot surge.

Not only does this restriction squash her attraction to you, but it also increases her stress. She does need to balance her words, but that is her work and you are not qualified to judge it. Instead, re-frame the words she's putting out into a larger context.

If she is surging her waves now, you can note that you love her femininity.

I live in a northern climate and love winter activities. Sometimes, however, this means that days are bitterly cold. This last winter, we had almost 48 hours with temperatures below -20F. It was easy to complain about those temperatures while forgetting that the northern location enables all the winter activities I love.

I offer men a simple model to use when their wives launch a barrage of negative words. "Those words are not about you—the words may have your name there, but it's still not about you. It's just about her feelings." No, this model isn't perfect, but this one is often valuable.

If that colossal assault wave of negativity is not actually about you, you are now free to act differently. You've probably had the experience of watching a similar negative assault wave directed toward a neutral third party. When the attack wasn't about you, you are free to comfort and empathize with your wife without the risk of being attacked. Here's an example of some strong words:

Victoria: "Bill, I can't believe you forgot to pay the electric bill! It's the only actual house task you agreed to take care of. Susan's husband, Randy, handles all their finances, and you can't even manage a single bill?! I'm so tired of you dropping the ball; I didn't want another child to care for! When are you ever going to grow up?"

Now, Bill has two choices. First, he can take it personally. There are plenty of personal attacks in Victoria's words that he could upset him. I suspect several of her claims aren't accurate; Bill could point those out, too. He could top it off by pointing out all the ways that Victoria acts like a child.

Alternatively, Bill can realize that these words aren't actually about him (even though they sure sound like it!) Instead of defending, Bill might realize that Victoria is most likely hurting. He can respond with empathy and compassion.

He might say, "Victoria, you're right that I did promise to take care of it, and I failed to do so. I can imagine you might feel hurt and maybe even a bit scared that you can't depend on me. I don't want you to be scared!"

Treat all verbal storms as not being about you. Respond with empathy and love. Detach your feelings and ego so that, in the moment, you can be all about loving your wife. You do not need to agree with things that are not true. Here's another example:

Her: "You never clean up, and I must do everything around here!"

Him: "It sounds like maybe you're feeling alone and don't have a team?"

In this example, he neither agreed with the core of her claim nor did he argue. He instead stepped around the attack and went for empathy with her heart. It is much easier to make this step if you realize the words are not about you.

Do not overanalyze your woman's words. They are not meant for intellectual analysis. They are simply an emotional exclamation. They are requesting love and tenderness, not logic.

Pour your love into her and let her ocean waves flow.

COMPLAINING

Complaining is not virtuous. When the Israelites complained against God, the seraph serpents resulted. Many Israelites died because of the complaints. I will discuss how to deal with complaining, but that does not mean it's a good thing.

Much of the struggle of marriage is learning how to best respond to the imperfections of others. You have many such imperfections that your wife must react to.

Also, note that you are not God. You do not get to send seraph serpents when your wife complains. Nor will pointing out the lack of virtue in complaining likely help much—particularly if offered at the wrong moment. Both men and women complain— but we tend to do it differently.

Imagine a wave on a mission to go somewhere. As it nears the beach, sand and rocks disrupt the flow. You can imagine the wave might be upset at the disturbance. The wave, however, might not be aware of exactly what got in the way. All it knows is that its plans have been thwarted! It starts to complain.

Often, when women complain, they do not correctly label the problem. Men aren't perfect at this either, but there tends to be more precision when living in Order. When women have a "big negative feeling," they take action. You may have noticed that if they don't know the real problem, they'll grab something nearby that fits the feeling. Men are often confused because even if they solve the "problem," the woman's feelings don't go away.

Remember that just because your woman is unhappy does not necessarily mean that you must take immediate and radical action. You must be the general in charge of the army—collect all the information carefully. Weigh her perspective heavily! Ultimately, however, you must make the decision that you deem best, even if it does not solve her unhappiness.

Women often have a much more sensitive "radar" than men, especially to emotional concerns. In temperament assessment, women are statistically more sensitive to negative emotions than men. Their radar may pick up a problem, but not correctly identify the disturbance.

COMPLAINT MODEL

One idea that may help you as a model is that women often do not know how to describe what is wrong. Like all models, this one isn't always true, but it may be helpful. When your wife attempts to articulate a problem, she may mislabel it. If you know this is a likely occurrence, it changes how you respond.

The first step is to gently dig a little deeper. "Tell me more about that feeling, what's going on? I want to know." Women often need to get many words out to find a better "fit" for the feeling. More of the words along the way will likely not be quite right, either. Sometimes, she needs to talk about it—and you can ask if that's what she needs (as discussed above). As she explores, she might start to communicate better what she perceives as the problem.

Let me offer some possible translations for various complaints. These are not definitive, but if your woman seems stuck, you might offer these as possible radar interpretations. Be careful; offering these may further fuel her negativity if she is in a bad mood.

Money Complaints

A common complaint women make is about money. Rarely, however, is money the problem. Money often represents potential. Perhaps your wife has made a story about what is supposed to happen. Jimmy must need sports lessons to be happier. To do this, however, the family needs more money. It's not about the money; she wants her son's happiness.

One good way to respond to complaints about money is to ask what the funds will enable. What good does she want to pursue that needs money? Explore that goal, and engage yourself in critical thinking as well. Is there an alternate route to that goal that does not require money but instead takes some time or attention?

Are you willing to offer that route as an alternative path? Often, a complaint about money is best addressed by stepping up and leading your wife with a good plan.

Children Complaints

Another common complaint topic is children. She may complain directly about the children or your interactions with them. Either way, her sensitive mother's heart likely worries that the child isn't thriving. She wants them to be happy now (remember the discussion about Present Love in Chapter 3).

In whatever form the complaint arrives, she likely wants you to be more involved with the children. Research overwhelmingly shows how critical a father's role is in a child's life. It is difficult to overstate. Whether consciously or not, she knows this need as well. Get more involved. Share your heart with your children, and love them. Yes, they are often boneheads that do foolish things. They're kids! Love them anyway, and you may find her complaining going down.

Sex Complaints

Sex is one topic that no man likes to hear his wife complain about. It may be a complaint about the frequency desired or any part of the process or lead-up. It's easy for a husband to interpret that complaint as an attack and take it personally. This response does not help.

A far better way to interpret a complaint about sex is that it isn't likely about the sex at all (unless it's something particular and detailed). Much more likely, it's a call to increase your love, affection, and cherishing of her outside the bedroom. Your woman wants to feel loved, pursued and wanted everywhere. A woman whose heart is filled outside the bedroom is much more likely to be happy in the bedroom. Where can you love and cherish her better?

Trivial Complaints

Complaints often seem to be about little or trivial things. This behavior can be very frustrating to a spouse. We value peace, and it's hard to understand why our spouse is fighting over something that feels trivial. When women fire off complaints over what seems trivial, there's a way to re-frame them as a man.

Again, a wave may not notice what got in the way, but that doesn't mean nothing is wrong. Instead of dismissing her complaint as trivial, be curious. What if there is something else, something more profound or fundamental, that you aren't living up to? Perhaps the complaint relates to a part of your life where you're not authentic. Maybe you're not honoring your word. The odds are high that her radar blip was catching something real, but perhaps not what she could articulate.

Overall, complaints are best viewed as the mystic rantings of an oracle rather than a scientific critique. Complaints are imperfect. They often leave room for you to defend. Rarely is that helpful. The Christian call is to humility. If you struggle with this idea, pray the Litany of Humility. Try to mean it. The better we respond with humility, the more likely we are to improve, and the more likely our relationship will improve.

WOMANLY WANTS

You may have thought before that your wife wants more things than you do. Many men are generally satisfied once they have met their basic needs. Many great men praise their wives for being a driving force behind them. Many unsuccessful men blame their wives for endless nagging because they never feel happy and content.

The question is not whether or not the waves keep coming and driving, but how are we men going to order our lives and families to channel that energy in a healthy way?

It is part of the feminine to surge and seek greater potential. Chaos itself is the source of life, novelty, and goodness. It's easy for Order to become complacent and be content with its Order. The feminine drive for more is intrinsically good, though, of course, like all good things, it can go awry in either direction or force.

If you merely oppose the waves and say, "No, nothing changes!" get ready to be unhappy. Similarly, denying the wave or trying to persuade the wave it's not supposed to flow will be equally unsuccessful. You must be ready to redirect the wave very carefully. Not only do you want to steer it in a way that she believes she'll get "what she wants" (more on that soon), but you also want to steer it so that she does get what she needs.

I have worked with many husbands who get frustrated and even upset when they consider the historic "wants" of their wives. "'All I want is just to own our home,' she used to say. Well, we do now, so why is she not happy??" Chaos is never satisfied with any fixed progress. It is a perpetual source of new energy, life, and direction. It rarely looks back in contemplation but maintains a drive to ever better those around.

Do not be surprised if your wife does not pause to express (what you think is) ample gratitude for the previous achievements. It is in her nature. You can certainly request that she slow down to celebrate with you, but she will want to resume the struggle. Her waves will come relentlessly—and be thankful for them. A vital part of the marital dynamic is lost if you do not have them.

WOMEN DO NOT KNOW WHAT THEY WANT.

I'm a crazy person. I like to go to the gym at 6 AM, which means I need to get up at 5:15. This requires me to go to bed early so I'm not a zombie for the day.

A few years ago, my wife was upset about how early I wanted to go to bed. She said, "I don't like it when you go to bed so early; adults don't need early bedtimes!" I was adamant that I wanted to go to bed early. We both went to bed that night early and upset.

The next day, we revisited this discussion. Instead of fighting, I asked her why bedtime was so important to her. After some digging, I discovered that what she really wanted was more time with me without little kids. Neither of us actually cared about the specific bedtime, but we had other needs. What a different perspective! I wish I had dug a little deeper the previous day.

I'm going to introduce another functional "model." Again, this model is not always true, but you may find it helpful. Women do not know what they want, but they do know how they want to feel. The feminine often guesses what worldly change will result in the desired emotional state. She then announces that she "wants" this worldly change.

Her guesses may sometimes be accurate, but they are often not. Your job as the masculine is not to be distracted or overwhelmed by the surface-level "want" but to dig deeper and seek to understand her heart. You might start by asking some questions.

"Why do you want this? What do you think will change for us and our family?"

Do her deeper desires align with yours? For example, if she says, "It will help this child to thrive," then ask yourself—do you want the child to thrive? Odds are yes, so start by agreeing with her intent. "That's important to me too! I also want this child to thrive." If you affirm her intent and express that you share it, the next stage might be easier.

If you do not share the desire (or perhaps simply not as strong of a desire), that's not necessarily a problem. In Chapter 8, I discussed that there is always a lower and higher desire for a partner for any activity, decision, or direction. That's OK! It is your job as a husband to evaluate if this direction is worthy of pursuing, even if it does not fully align with your desires.

Consider if there might be problems she has yet to foresee with her desired path. Consider if you can devise an alternate route to yield a higher likelihood of success. She will likely be more open to these thoughts if you align your desires.

The real key is not to get tied up in whatever she says she wants. She wants something deeper and will likely try another approach if it satisfies that more profound desire.

REQUESTS ARE OFTEN TESTS.

How often does your wife ask, "Do you love me?" Probably not very frequently—and for good reason. Unless a man is in the most horrible of moods, he will almost inevitably answer with "Yes!" So, what does the woman learn by asking that question? Very little.

Over time, whether consciously or unconsciously, women have learned that some questions are best asked indirectly.

Often, requests are an indirect way to ask questions like "Am I still important to you?" or "Do you still treasure me?" The actual request may seem silly and frivolous. However, it's not about the actual request but the feelings, fears, and insecurities underneath.

If you have never watched the popular YouTube video "It's not about the nail," I encourage you to do so. It captures the frustration often experienced by husbands. To her, it isn't about the nail. It is, but the deeper emotional issue is simply more important.

Let me try to explain this. I recently read a study that asked people how often or frequently they genuinely fear they are about to die.

The average man said he was genuinely afraid he was about to die only a handful of times in his entire life, and he usually had a pretty epic story to go with each. By contrast, the average woman said it was several times *per week*. Think about that for a second.

Before puberty, boys and girls have roughly the same sensitivity to negative emotion, measured by psychological temperament tests called "neuroticism." After puberty, however, women show a significant increase in neuroticism that men do not. Some speculate that this is a necessary change to help keep the vulnerable mother-infant combination safe. It certainly has some unfortunate side effects.

When a situation that might cause a negative emotion happens to a woman (say, a funny noise on a dark street at night), she, on average, responds with much more negative emotion (fear) than a man might. A man might feel slightly nervous or perhaps even scared. A woman might be terrified, believing that she might die.

This reality permeates an adult woman's experience. It creates fear and insecurity in a woman that is often very different from men. Men experience their fears and insecurity, but usually about their capability, worth, or whether they can be loved—much less about their physical safety. Men often seek indirect ways to affirm their fears, and so do women. Both genders commonly misunderstand these indirect requests.

A common way that men seek affirmation of their goodness is through sex. The parallel is women asking for things like "planning the date night for the two of them" or "finding novel things to do with her." It feels impossible sometimes to please your wife's requests because it's not really about the request; it's about her fear that you no longer value, cherish, or desire her as a complete person.

Instead of fighting over whether or not your date idea was good enough for her, seek her heart by exploring these deeper fears.

Assure her, with a powerful emotional presence, that you value, cherish, and desire her—and not only sexually. Value her wisdom, kindness, compassion, mothering, etc. A woman is also afraid of being reduced to a sexual object.

Affirm, praise, and cherish her. Pour out a strong emotion into these words. You'll find that these seemingly impossible requests might get a bit easier.

SHE IS TESTING YOUR STRENGTH.

Women have always faced an interesting problem when selecting a spouse. If she chooses one who is too dangerous, he might turn on her, and she won't be safe. Alternatively, if she chooses one who is too weak and powerless, he won't be able to defend her from the predators that circle.

This contradictory need for a spouse to both be "safe" and "dangerous" at the same time creates a universal challenge for women. When young, many women pursue a "bad boy" style relationship to emphasize the "danger" of a mate. When he hurts her, she realizes that she also needs safety. Her next relationship may be a mild-mannered, safe man, but she soon realizes she isn't attracted to him. As she ages, she starts to realize that she needs a "dangerous" man who is constrained somehow to also be "safe" specifically with her. The most common constraint is a moral one reinforced by religion.

Unfortunately, much of this female evaluation is taking place subconsciously. If a man is not "dangerous" enough, she likely finds low sexual attraction. Suppose he is not "safe" enough. In that case, she'll hesitate to commit to a long-term relationship, but she is unsure why. Even worse, this evaluation is repeated frequently throughout the evolving relationship. She may initially find a man attractive enough (dangerous) and yet still want to get married (safe).

Still, as the relationship progresses, her husband stops caring for himself and loses his passion and drive (dangerous). In this scenario, she may find her sexual attraction decreasing.

A married man can be very frustrated by this decreased attraction. A large young family is complicated to balance with the needs of an early career. He may justify his decreased energy and passion because he "has to be responsible and care for everyone." A woman rarely responds well to justification and defensive behaviors, especially if she doesn't understand her decreased attraction. One way for any spouse to grow is to realize the need to do something even if one doesn't "feel" like doing it. However, you can't force her to grow. You will not help by pointing out her lack of charity and pouting.

Sometimes, her evaluation will show that she is no longer "safe." In extreme cases, this can lead her to separate herself. In lesser cases, this can sometimes lead to marital coldness and separation. In my work, I usually find this to be a secondary condition only after a primary breach has occurred in the marriage. Because of the breach, both spouses become angry and hurt each other, resulting in the evaluation of "not safe."

This section will focus on the need to be "dangerous." Your woman wants you to be strong enough to be dangerous. She wants you to defend her from in-laws, community members, the children (particularly boys), and herself. The problem is, how does she make this assessment? She does it indirectly (again) out of necessity.

If a wife asked her husband, "Are you safe?" He would, of course, answer, "Yes." If she asked him, "Are you strong and dangerous enough to protect me?" He might not understand, but he would not claim to be weak. When you encounter these requests, try to view them not at face value but as an expression of her deep female need to evaluate this difficult equation.

My wife often asks me to call companies when we disagree with their actions. She also asks me to respond "no" to an in-law request when she fears upsetting them. Those examples are fairly straightforward.

The tougher ones are her requests that I must say "no" to be authentic to what I believe to be true. Let me demonstrate this idea with two more stories, one about my failure and one about my success.

After my wife and I married, I discovered her grandmother was a bit interesting. She had filled her house with delicate and expensive trinkets and had little tolerance for young children. Furthermore, "appearance" was often more important than actual "connection" in her house. Many events were about posturing and appeasing, politics were rampant, and gifts were signals of approval, not love.

Well, one particular Christmas when we had two little children, her grandmother suddenly announced that she wanted the whole family to go to her house for Christmas dinner. We had already had a difficult and tiring day, but, even worse, we suspected there would be a dramatic display of favoritism via Christmas presents for some other grandkids. I did not want anything to do with this upcoming mess.

I suspect my wife's most significant motivation was a genuine love of her family (though vanity is a struggle for many women). I knew, deep down, however, that it would not be good for our family to attend this spontaneous event. My wife strongly wanted to go, threatening to go with just the kids if necessary. I caved. I justified my attendance with the idea of not abandoning the children to madness without some amount of protection.

The event went poorly, and much of what I feared did come to pass. On the way home, everyone was upset. As the fighting escalated, I made several choice observations about her vanity, selfishness, and lack of willingness to prioritize her new family. I was mad at her for the event, or at least I thought. Deep down, I was angry for not doing what I knew was right.

As with the story of our tire-chasing puppy, it's pretty common that when a husband fails to do what is right, he gets angry at his wife. It's very powerful to ask oneself why exactly one is mad. How much might it be about my actions?

Alternatively, let's consider a win of mine. At one point, my wife wanted to move to a different house that I knew wasn't right for us. She had many reasons, stories, and feelings about why we should move. She was 100% committed to this move and believed it was right.

I believed 100% that it was wrong. We both prayed about it, and I continued to get the message not to make the move. When I firmly decided "no," she was sad, upset, and grumpy for months. I didn't know it, but I had earned her respect. When new information came months later that affirmed my decision, I was shocked at how well she handled it. My decision reaffirmed that I was strong enough to keep her safe, even from herself. She still talks about this decision today as a positive moment in our marriage.

Of course, my goal is not to encourage you to say "no" to your wife for the fun of it. Instead, first, do your diligent prayer and reflection about an issue. If you sincerely believe the answer is "no," stick to that answer even in the face of her negative emotions. You must be strong enough to lead. If you can withstand her negative emotions, it's a sign you're strong enough to keep her safe. Deep down, she knows that her feelings come with risk.

A man who will be the order in his marriage and guide the waves of his wife's emotions will increase his attractiveness and become the man his wife desperately seeks. It may seem counterintuitive to you. Lean into being the rock, being the order. Your wife is desperate for that strength but likely does not know how to ask for it. She is trying as hard as she can to seek it in the most efficient way she knows—even though it may seem very painful to you. She must know that she is safe from the outside and within.

SHE DOESN'T WANT TO BE NUMBER ONE.

All humans are prideful. We all want to be the most important—especially in our minds. Yet, a Christian must acknowledge his shortcomings, weaknesses, and sins. Children insist they get what they want and have no clue how badly that will work out. As we become adults, we realize our will is faulty and leads to problems.

Our wives likely realize their will is faulty and will lead to problems, but there is a further complication. When she leans into her femininity, she realizes (at least subconsciously) that her Chaos cannot be allowed to be in charge. If you do not bring your masculinity into play to balance her feminine Chaos, she will shift into masculinity herself.

Women want permission to be Chaos, to be waves. Part of that permission is believing they will be cared for, led, and directed. When you are the Order, it allows her to lean into her Chaos. When you are the rock, she gets to be entirely a wave. She cannot be fully feminine if she is number one or in the lead.

There are two concerns you must bring to your wife's attention. The first is the Lord. Intellectually, we know that God must be first, but what does that mean?

Practically, it means that when your wife advocates for anything grave in contrast to the faith, you must choose the faith. You must refuse if she advocates that you eat steaks and break your fast on Ash Wednesday on a whim.

If she wants to go on birth control and you discern there is not sufficient medical need (this is another book in itself), then you must not agree.

To place God first means to give up what we want most when it conflicts with God's plan. Men commonly face this tension when their wives have strong negative emotions over an issue we cannot agree with. Strong negative emotions in our wives are very painful to men! When this occurs over an issue of the faith, add this suffering to your cross. Your wife wants this—even if she may not express it well. Later, when the current emotional storm has passed, she will value your authenticity and strength.

The second you must be willing to overrule your wife is when you and she are in a deadlock. Pray and discern first—you may be wrong. If you are unwilling to overrule your wife, you will be weak.

I shared two stories about a deadlock with my wife in the previous section. When a man believes deep down that he knows the right action, but it conflicts with his wife's perspective, he is in a dangerous situation. If he caves to her will out of fear, she will resent him for it. Even if it works out, she has married a weak man. She will not respect you or be attracted to weakness or fear.

A common struggle for many men is balancing their obligations to their job and their families. Obviously, a wife does not want her husband to frequently skip work to help her if it means losing her job. Yet their behavior often does not indicate awareness of that potential. I've talked to many men who genuinely believe that their wife wants to be the first priority. Indeed, a wife should be a higher priority than a job. So, how do we men navigate these traps?

As with every other decision in life, prayer is our secret weapon. I often teach men the concept of a "micro-prayer."

We don't have time to jump into Adoration for 15 minutes for most decisions. "Should I go home early?" "Should I stay late today to finish this project?" Rather than squeezing your brain to try to find the optimal solution, turn to the Lord. Take ten seconds and ask Him, "Lord, what do you want me to do in this situation?" Abandon your own goals and desires and seek to serve Him.

When a man places the Lord's will above his wife's, he is much better able to weather her storm of dissatisfaction. You will fail in this balance and misunderstand Him occasionally—especially when your ego or agenda gets in the way. When you do, apologize to her and to the Lord. You serve Him first, her second. Only when you fix your eyes on Jesus can you do the impossible and float on the water in the middle of her Chaos storm.

Chaos is sometimes loud, distracting, and potentially even destructive. A man who is not confident in his conviction and the Lord's guidance will often cave before the chaotic onslaught of his wife's femininity. Despite seeming to get her way, she is not happy. Instead, stand firm in your faith, listening to the Lord. Pray, read, and discern regularly. Listen well to your wife, weigh her perspective highly, and lead her boldly!

SHE WANTS TO REST IN YOUR STRENGTH.

It might not seem like it, but your wife wants to know that you are strong so that she can rest in that strength. A well-directed wave will feel safer than an uncontrolled wave. You can see the importance of this safety by watching what women find attractive in men.

Men value physical features more than women do. Women do, however, find certain male physical features attractive. Consider famous male actors in movies. They are generally physically fit and relatively muscular. They are also highly confident and sophisticated. Their overall impression is one of great strength and ability to accomplish their goals. Women like this.

When a woman believes a man is strong and capable, she does not need to be scared or anxious. Because women are sensitive to negative emotions, the need to be safe, taken care of, and protected is critical! Even if she may not be able to fully let go of all anxiety and worry (that is her journey and work), his capability gives her permission to relax at least.

One word of caution: your wife wants to feel safe. If you are super strong, but she feels like you are dangerous, then your strength doesn't help her. In my own marriage, I've built out biceps and quads that are pretty impressive, but when my wife views me as "danger," my muscles don't comfort her at all. When she feels safe with me, she calms down and is more enjoyable to be around.

Do not be too quick to dismiss the importance of your physical strength. It is less important than emotional or spiritual strength, but it matters. Lean into all your strengths, and become a man who is strong enough for her to rest in. As her energy is no longer required for worry, she might have enough for another activity you appreciate more!

DON'T SUGGEST SHE SOLVE HER EMOTIONAL PROBLEMS.

At first, this might sound like I'm giving women a pass on their emotional issues. Indeed, many coaches for women (my wife included) will encourage their female clients to deal with and regulate their uncontrolled emotions. My point here is that it is not optimal for you to suggest to your wife that she regulate her emotional problems.

Your role in the relationships is to be the Order, the rock, the stability. When you tell her to deal with her stuff (even if it's something she should be dealing with), you ask her to step into the role of Order. There's nothing wrong with a woman stepping into Order or a man stepping into Chaos. You do not, however, want her to step into that role within the context of your intimate marriage relationship!

Most husbands I have worked with have attempted to ask their wives to solve their emotions, and with rare exceptions, that goes poorly. If you've been married more than a year, you probably have your examples when such a request didn't work.

When she loses control, rather than describing the many ways she has lost control (and likely expressing a strong desire that she get her "fecal matter" together), instead take control of the conversation and lead her into another mood yourself.

Take her hand, look into her eyes, and affirm your love for her and her safety. Affirm your desire that children be well cared for, or whatever the issue is. Give her a hug or perhaps a bump with your belly so that she can feel your masculine presence. Use your physical presence to steer the energy of her wave into a better place.

Many of the "emotional problems" expressed by a woman operating in her feminine state are not accurate. They are a radar indication of strong emotions but are not necessarily fully pinned on specific events and actions in the real world. Instead of asking her to become masculine, be masculine yourself. Steer the energy of the wave somewhere productive.

Encourage her to find good, holy female friends who strive to improve. It is their job to help encourage your wife to solve her emotional problems. They will do it in a totally foreign way to how you think. If you are curious, watch a group of women discuss an emotional issue. If you listen to what they say—it may sound crazy. That's OK; they're speaking a different language than you know.

Be the Order for your wife. Create a structure for her, guide her waves. Create spaces for her to be feminine and encourage her to be friends with other women. Do not try to take upon yourself a job you cannot do.

IT'S NOT ABOUT YOUR TRACK RECORD—IT'S ONLY ABOUT THIS MOMENT

A common complaint husbands have is that their wives do not seem to give them "credit" for what they've accomplished. Husbands will work hard to achieve a significant task. Then, with minimal (or no) acknowledgment or gratitude, his wife is simply on to asking for (or nagging about) the next item on her problem list.

A good friend once complained to me about this. A few years prior, his wife said that all she wanted was to own her own home—a home that was big enough for their growing family. They purchased a home that fit their family very well. They had a reasonable down payment, a good interest rate, and a plan to pay it successfully over time. Rather than being happy, she complained about the kids' schooling, the car, etc. He questioned, "Why can't I ever win?"

A wave exists purely in the "now." Neither past nor future is essential to Chaos. The feminine lives in the feelings of the moment. The feelings may be caused by considering past events or future projections, but they are all about what she feels "right now." Perhaps she felt OK about the schooling plan yesterday, but after one of her friends suggested a problem, she thinks it is horrible now.

If you object by describing the discrepancy between "before" and "now," you will not win. Your wife will perceive that you are arguing with her about her feelings—trying to "take them away from her." One effective way to get a woman to dig in is to suggest her feelings aren't valid. You might be right about the events, but her perception makes her feelings inarguable. Even if they are negative (and perhaps present a skewed reality), they are her feelings. It takes a lot of maturity for a woman to separate feelings from reality.

Allow your wife to swirl in Chaos a bit. Allow her waves to surge to and fro. It's OK that she has an immense feeling now that isn't pleasant. It's OK if she suggests that a big action must be taken right now that you know is wrong. All things pass, including feelings. Rather than fight the feelings, validate that she feels a certain way. This validation by no means necessitates that you agree with a proposed action.

"I see you are feeling scared, and I can understand that you are worried about [whatever.] I also want to make sure that works out. Let's pray about it and see what we think tomorrow." Her feelings are probably picking up a problem somewhere. They may need to be more accurate in the magnitude and specific positioning of the problem—but it does not help you to argue about it!

Allow her to live in the moment. Whether she is ignoring your previous achievements or projecting excessive doom in the future, do not try to take her feelings away. Instead, acknowledge her feelings and take charge of the situation with love, kindness, and tenderness. Lead to the deeper desires of her heart.

Her feelings will surge again; if you build the proper structure of Order, they will flow to a better place.

Over the years, I have heard many statements from both my wife and my clients' wives that, if interpreted literally, would be terrifying!

"I never want to have sex again."

"I really hate you."

"I'll never trust you."

"You're the worst."

"I cannot depend on you."

If a man were to say these sentences to us, that would be a long-term problem. When our wives say them, however, they may simply be an indication of her feelings in that moment.

In other moments, you may have excelled in any of those categories. In this one, however, she feels that you aren't. That's it. Don't treat it as anything more. Do not try to defend—you cannot win because you're arguing something different from what she means.

DON'T BE AFRAID TO MEET YOUR WOMAN IN THE ENERGY SHE IS IN. SHE WANTS YOUR FULL POTENTIAL.

Because they are easily misused, we are afraid of some of our God-given desires and drives. For example, the desire to make a lot of money or have exciting sex can easily lead to sin. Although God created these to be good, we often seek them incorrectly. This danger, however, does not mean they are always wrong. All desires can lead to holiness when followed at the correct times and in the proper ways.

God has chosen this spouse for you. One of her jobs is to help call forth your potential. She will get into a mood that may surprise you or perhaps seem scary. Lean into that mood (when it is not sinful, of course.)

If she wants to be excited about a big project and you agree it's a good plan, join her in her excitement! If she wants a powerful bedroom romp in a way that doesn't break the teachings of the church, then match that energy, too.

Remember that one of man's downfalls is inaction. Like Adam in the Garden of Eden, we are tempted to sit and rest without engaging. Your wife, among many other jobs, is there to help provide energy and motivation to your marriage. Use that energy! God may be calling you to get your butt into motion.

Even our "dark" energy can be used for the glory of God when used in the proper context and for the correct reasons. Perhaps she is upset about an injustice at church, but you are too conflict-averse to engage with the pastor. While remaining kind and respectful, acknowledge the injustice and seek a remedy. Your wife's feminine energy is there to help jolt you into action. It will sometimes feel uncomfortable, but it may be what you need!

PRAISE HER LAVISHLY

In the previous chapter, I proposed that one of your jobs as a man is to call forth the good in others. This concept is of particular significance when applied to your wife. It is still true that you have the creative capacity and thus are responsible for calling forth the good in her, but there are also two additional considerations. First, you have spiritual authority over her. This authority increases your duty and obligation. Second, you must consider her unique needs not only as a woman but as a woman who has given herself entirely to you.

Spiritual authority is a real and powerful concept. In Matthew 16:19, Jesus gives Peter the keys to the kingdom of heaven; whatever he binds on earth is bound in heaven, etc. With great power comes great responsibility. Peter's successors, the Popes, have had tremendous power and responsibility because of this legitimate authority. You also have spiritual authority over your wife and children.

Your authority is not the equivalent of the Pope's, but it is probably more significant than you normally consider.

When you speak over your wife, it does affect change. If you speak positively, the change is positive. If you speak negatively, don't expect your life to get any better. One day, you will stand in front of the Lord, and He will ask you to account for how you have used this authority. Were you a good steward of your wife?

Consider also what a woman needs emotionally. I spoke earlier that, statistically, women are more sensitive to negative emotions than men. One of the side effects is that they benefit more from large quantities and quality of praise than men sometimes do. A woman's mind often creates negative stories that pose a danger to her.

Imagine what life must have been like when culture was simply a small tribe living in the woods. If the clan rejected a man, he could live independently and perhaps find another tribe to join. Unlike a man, however, a woman who was rejected becomes easy and desirable prey for predatory men. Women's fear of societal rejection is much closer to death than for men. Indeed, women are generally more afraid of public embarrassment than men.

If it is dangerous for a woman to be rejected by society, it is even more dangerous for her to be rejected by her husband. He is the one man she has given everything to. She cannot have it back. Throughout history, if a husband and wife separated, she struggled more than he did. He could provide for himself and look for a new spouse while she struggled with both tasks.

When you lavish praise upon your wife, you provide evidence against this deep and primal fear in her. Of course, she has her work, but you can do a ton to help her. A wife who feels safe and secure will likely feel more free to live fully femininely and lavish love on her husband. When you lavish praise upon her, you help combat the fear of rejection and banishment by her husband and society.

One final note: there is a big difference between legitimate praise and indulging her in vanity. While vanity differs from pride, it can be almost as sneaky and damaging. Praise her in a way that does not compare her to other women but notes the good in her. God has indeed blessed her greatly; there is much to work with! Here are a couple of short examples:

"You are so much prettier than all the other women!" (vain) vs. "You are so beautiful, I find you stunning!" (praise)

"You're amazing because you can cook better," as opposed to "I really love how you cook."

Vanity is a struggle for everyone, but do not let that be a reason for you not to lavish praise upon your wife. Praise her in a way that calls forth the good. There is so much ground to work on there.

CHAPTER TEN
PRACTICAL STEPS FOR SELF-CARE

Modern humans have a funny perspective on self-care. We all have basic needs, but we only believe that caring for some of them is appropriate. For example, has anyone ever criticized you for taking the time to breathe an average, typical breath of air? Probably not. While I have sometimes been criticized about eating, most people generally understand it's essential.

As a culture, we have other needs that we do not treat as necessary. We need silence, emotional connection, reading good materials or some intellectual new material, exercise, and much more. Yet, so many people will criticize those who try to pursue those needs.

When you get on an airplane, you've probably heard the typical safety speech: "Secure your own mask before helping another." This guideline is not a selfish philosophy; it's common sense. If you pass out due to a lack of air, you're totally unable to help anyone at all. You must care for your basic needs first.

This final chapter is devoted to less apparent needs if you want to thrive as a man. It's not obvious how quiet, prayer, and learning new things are essential to thriving as a human. Similarly, these ideas may not be obvious—but live them anyway.

THE BASICS

You likely already know much about what your body, heart, mind, and soul need. The purpose of this book is not to be a general health guide. I'm going to cover a few basics very quickly. You also probably already know what you need to do for these if they're a problem:

- Eat a healthy diet. If you don't know what this means for you, research and experiment. Most of us know one step we could take to improve here.

- Get enough sleep. The data about the value of sleep is overwhelming. Just do it.

- Get exercise. It's the same as with sleep. Just do it.

- Do not indulge in vices. You know deep down if drinking, entertainment, or whatever your vice is, is going too far. Get it back into order, or cut it out entirely.

- Take care of your primary health. Too many men pridefully refuse to go to a doctor if they aren't well.

- Get to confession monthly. Or more.

- Attend mass every Sunday, more if possible.

- Be faithful to God's commands. Avoid mortal sin relentlessly.

If you are struggling in any of these areas, take action. If you don't know what to do, seek help. Many in your circle of acquaintances and community know how to help. It's OK if you're not perfect—it's also OK if the first step you take doesn't solve everything—or maybe it doesn't work. Keep trying.

The heart of this chapter will be about how to care for your masculinity and masculine self.

DO NOT DEPOLARIZE

Polarity is something you must maintain. I've talked about how important it is for proper attraction and marital interaction. Your wife's energy will go destructive if you are not the Order to guide it. It's also important, however, in your job, in your friendships, even as a father. Your family, friends, and even your community need your masculinity.

When you work, you will inspire others to follow you better if you live in confidence and order. You will be in better control of your reactions and better able to analyze your problems as they arise. You will likely find yourself leading up as well as down. Masculine energy can attract men and women toward a business goal or financial objective.

When you are forming friendships with other men, your masculinity will signal to other masculine men that you are worth their time in friendships. You have probably noticed that you hesitate to share too much when confronted by a very feminine man. We men are naturally a bit hesitant around an overly feminized man.

For a long time, the typical response about such a man was that he needed a good kick to the bum to get him moving. Perhaps you currently find yourself in this position. If so, I hope this book provides the kick for you.

There are moments to be feminine. There are also moments to be soft and tender while still masculine. A man can be well-ordered but still very soft and tender. Imagine if your daughter, or perhaps a niece or close relative, was crying. If you had to help comfort her, she would want to hear your rock-like stability. Of course, you would speak softly and with comfort and encouragement. You would do it from a place of Order, helping to frame the world for her.

While remaining strongly polarized, you can be gentle or firm, tender or stern. The masculine energy you bring to the situation will attract men and women alike. Nobody likes a lukewarm individual. Even Our Lord specifically rejects the lukewarm in Revelation.

There is one situation where it is not only OK but sometimes even beneficial to depolarize. If you are struggling with a big problem and don't know what to do, find another man to discuss it with. Do not share this sort of problem with your wife. If your Order is weak, it will challenge her safety. Instead, find a man who is wise, faithful, open to discussion, and, if possible, has gone through a similar situation himself. Ask him for an hour. Go out for coffee, tea, or whatever. Share your innermost thoughts with him without reservation. Listen to his feedback.

As a man, your life is meant to be one of battle, of challenge. God intends you to gird your loins, pick up your armor, and go into battle. Sometimes that even needs to be done lovingly against your brother's sins as you help him (gently) to see where he is erring. Ours is not the way of the feminine—women have a different sort of pain and sacrifice.

Remain firm in your polarized masculinity. Bring the fullness of your masculine energy in whatever form best serves all you interact with. If you find yourself depolarizing, do the following:

- Lean into your faith

- Go to confession

- Spend more time in prayer

- Consider fasting

- Consider daily Mass

- Speak with a priest or spiritual director

- Consult men who are wise, faithful, and experienced

- Add your sufferings to your cross. Pick it up and follow Him as best as you are able.

- Surrender everything you cannot directly control. He will not test you beyond what you can bear.

Our three boys were born within a three year period. For each pregnancy, my wife was restricted to pretty severe bed rest for many months. After each birth, her medical condition improved, but she was focused on caring for the new infant.

As a result, for over three years, I lived in chronic overwhelm trying to build a business while also caring for multiple young children and my semi-incapacitated wife.

Not surprisingly, I depolarized pretty severely. I went into survival mode, trying to get just the critical basics done for each party in need. My personal care definitely dropped. While this is understandable to a certain extent, the damage was far more significant than I would have expected.

It was during the pregnancy of our sixth child that my wife and I experienced a pretty big emotional rift. While no doubt due to many factors (including the very significant amount of physical pain she was in), one factor for sure that I contributed to was my lack of polarization.

She felt much less attraction, and sex was not at all a desirable activity at that time. While we both were in survival mode, this break between us removed our ability to take comfort from being together in the mess.

We are still working to recover from this time. I wonder, if I had stayed more strongly masculine, how that might have affected that pregnancy.

ATTRACTION

Part of self-care is having a healthy vision of male attraction. Let's use diet as an example: If you do not know what a healthy diet is (and that is indeed a topic of much debate currently), it is hard to eat in a healthy way.

Imagine if a man believed protein was unhealthy and chose a diet with little or no protein. He would soon start to struggle with basic tasks as his muscles rebelled. He would likely begin to crave protein-rich foods in a way that might upset him. He might even feel guilty for that craving.

Similarly, you need a healthy understanding of sexual attraction. This force is potent and often disrupts even the strongest of men. We need to be specific about what is sinful and what is not. Many men beat themselves up and shame themselves over a natural and unavoidable attraction. Life becomes very difficult.

First, we need to define what is sinful. Sin involves action. This action may be internal to our mind alone or external. It may be a wrong action that was done or a good action that was omitted. There are many ways in which our will influences our actions. Once the will is involved, sin is possible.

Attraction, by itself, does not involve an act of the will. Now, one possible action of the will is to indulge that attraction. Whether you keep looking at the pretty girl, or merely replay the video in your mind of when she bent over in front of you, both actions are sinful. Your initial attraction, however, was different.

As you go through life, you will find yourself powerfully attracted to women (and perhaps men) in ways that may startle or surprise you. One typical example of when this causes a problem is when a married man is attracted to another woman or when an older man finds a younger woman attractive.

These men may shame themselves in their heads (if not worse) for these "improper" attractions. This same problem frequently happens to men who struggle with same-sex attraction.

It is a funny thing in the therapy world that the sexual stories about which we feel the most shame may also contain the most power to bring healing and light into our lives. This process is more complex than this book allows, but it is extremely important. If you suffer from a great deal of shame, I strongly encourage you to seek help. Bringing healing into this area of your life will affect all of your relationships, not only your marriage.

ATTRACTION TO YOUNGER WOMEN

Young women possess a natural, vibrant, and intoxicating form of feminine energy. Even if you are not sexually attracted, you may find yourself drawn towards this energy. Perhaps you are more likely to laugh; maybe you light up with a smile. Your chest may feel lighter, and your mood may improve. This energy affects the heart just as much as the genitals. This attraction is not sinful; it is the way God designed the genders to work.

When you encounter a younger beauty, praise God for the goodness of His creation. I was present on a job site once when a good Catholic man noticed some women walking by immodestly. He turned his eyes toward heaven and exclaimed, "What amazing and beautiful work You have done here, Lord!" His eyes were up until the women were past and out of sight.

Even your daughters will bring delight and joy into your life that is not sexual but is an expression of their powerful feminine energy. If you have daughters, one helpful trick of the mind when confronted by a different beautiful woman is to imagine that she is like your daughter. The youthful, raw Chaos and powerful waves of that energy are something to be appreciated, but never translated into sinful actions. You want to protect that goodness, not consume or damage it!

In an even more accurate way, every woman and girl (even your wife) is really God's daughter, and He wants you to care for them as He intended. By all means, appreciate the beauty and power of the feminine energy that God creates.

In a similar way, appreciate the masculine vitality and energy that your sons (and all men) possess. These goods can be appreciated and praised without sinful action.

When you are attracted to younger women, do not be ashamed. Act with honor and do not sin. If need be, leave the situation or avert your eyes. Like the man at the job site, it may be enough to keep your eyes elsewhere until the moment has passed. Stop shaming yourself for mere attraction; instead, practice chaste and virtuous habits and thoughts. As you grow in chastity, it will be easier to notice when your heart and will are tempted towards sinful actions. Oppose those actions relentlessly.

FORBIDDEN ATTRACTIONS AND SHAME

I have coached multiple Catholic men who suffer from same-sex attraction while pursuing purity. I've also coached men who are addicted to pornography, have had affairs, and many other sexual impurities. Every man I've worked with at some point has brought up a moment where he experienced sexual attraction in a way that he thought was "forbidden," "unacceptable," or "terrible." Our response to these attractions is critical.

First, let me address another typical case of sexual attraction that commonly causes shame: attraction to younger female body shapes. Because this is so common, it deserves a moment to break it apart. You may skip a few paragraphs if this doesn't apply to you. Let me approach this scientifically.

Much of sexual attraction (for both genders) is based upon a subconscious assessment of fertility and the likelihood of successfully raising offspring. There are two primary approaches found in men. Data shows that roughly 75% of men are attracted to large breasts, hips, and buttocks on a woman. These are signs of fertility that she is likely to be able to give birth safely and feed a child successfully. About 25% of men, however, are attracted to more petite and younger features in a woman. These are also signs of fertility, as younger women are much more likely to survive pregnancy and undergo successful childbirth.

Here's the problem: there's an obvious severe downside when this approach goes too far. It is common for men who are attracted to younger features to view this with shame and disgust.

Let me be very clear: Sexual sin can be very grave and often has the potential to cause tremendous damage. Some temptations must never be indulged, even in the littlest way, due to the potential damage. It is not the attraction that makes a man evil, but his actions.

For comparison, most people have had a suicidal impulse, which must be opposed. Similarly, improper sexual action must be rejected entirely. It is not the attraction to kill that makes one a murderer, no matter how much my children frustrate me. God built you with the attractions you started with. You have further developed them throughout your life (often unconsciously). The question now is, how will you respond?

Attraction itself is not wrong. Whether it is to another man, a younger woman, a woman other than your wife, or any other forbidden target, the action determines sinfulness. Do not shame yourself because of an attraction.

Shame is a destructive, though typical, response in many men. This shame can damage relationships with family and with God. Most men who feel this shame for any of the examples given discover this damage much later. Do not be ashamed of how God has made you. He has a plan to bring all things to a greater good. Instead, focus on making your actions holy.

HOW TO HANDLE ATTRACTIONS THAT OUGHT NOT TO BE PURSUED

The saint is not a man who was never tempted by sin or attracted to a wrong action. Instead, the saint is the man who overcame those temptations—or at least repented and fought anew when he fell. Responding with chastity to sexual attraction is a challenge for all men. Here are some practical ways to do it.

1. Reframe the situation.

So often, our ability to resist temptation and attraction depends on how the problem is framed. Imagine you were tempted to do an immoral act with another woman, but everyone you know in the world was right there staring at you two. Alternatively, imagine she was the daughter of a close friend; you'd want to protect her!

When you are tempted to do something, remember that not only are your guardian angel, the Lord, and all the saints currently watching you but everything will one day be made known. See each person you might hurt as being someone's loved one. Remember that when we commit sin, we injure ourselves more than whoever we hurt. No matter what good you receive (and yes, there is some good), it is always less than the harm done to yourself and any other person. There is no victimless sin.

Ask yourself, how would God see this situation? She is His daughter. Protect her as if she were your own!

2. Tolerate no sinful actions, period.

So often, we men like to draw these imaginary lines: "This far is OK, but beyond it is bad." Intellectually, we likely know the words of Christ in Matthew 5 about committing adultery in our hearts. The devil's first goal is often not to get a man into physical adultery but merely to tolerate lustful small steps.

Consider the word "tolerate." For many years, there was a great deal of political energy behind a movement of "tolerance." We were told to tolerate other ideas, behaviors, and ways of life.

Let me offer a contrast: Imagine you had a fabulous meal for your birthday with your favorite foods and drinks. Your friends, wife, and loved ones are there. Do you "tolerate" this meal?

We tolerate pain. We tolerate suffering and mistakes. To "tolerate" a thing means there is something wrong. Yet, when it comes to lustful eyes and thoughts, we men sometimes think we can "tolerate" them, maybe because the fight against them is just too hard. The irony is that allowing only a little bit of lust is an even more brutal fight than allowing none at all.

Sometimes men get confused about where a dream ends and a fantasy begins. If you have a sexual dream while asleep (whether it involves release or not), there is no sin. You have no act of the will involved in this.

Imagine you wake in the middle of such a dream. For the first few moments, your will is very limited. As you wake further, you are morally obligated to engage your will against the fantasy. Sinful begins when you choose to continue the internal movie. Do not tolerate fantasies. They are not harmless.

Your attractions are powerful and real, but do not always point you in the right direction. Draw a hard line against lustful actions. Refuse to tolerate even the littlest bit.

Yes, you will likely fall in small (and sometimes not small) ways into lust. Never tolerate them. Repent quickly and return to your efforts towards chastity.

3. *Understand the emotions that are draining your strength.*

Commonly, we men will do well in our struggles against lust until negative emotions swamp us. Perhaps you are feeling deeply rejected by your wife. Maybe you feel crushed by your parents and rejected by your peers. Possibly, you painfully lost your job.

When we men feel overwhelmed by negative emotions, we commonly give up our struggles in other areas also. This behavior makes sense in the case of a physical ailment; the last time I had a flu bug, I stayed within a few feet of a toilet. I was in no shape to go into battle. When we get sick, we generally will lie low until we feel better. The difference is that when we are overwhelmed by negative emotions, we often do not deal with them—allowing them to linger and fester. I have known men (myself included) who have allowed negative feelings and thoughts to fester for decades.

Men must get back into the battle. Knowing this, we seek a doctor if a physical condition disables us. We must treat emotional conditions similarly. Proper emotional care is challenging to find; professional opinions and approaches vary widely. Therapists have failed many men, some destructively. After enough failures, we men decide to ignore the problem.

Instead of running to a therapist (though if the issue is genuinely trauma-related, a good therapist can change your life forever), consider the alternatives presented in this book. Most of all, take your emotional wounds in their raw form into prayer. Too many men believe that cold, detached, and formal prayers are the only way to pray. The rosary is amazing and brings great graces—but it is not the only type of prayer. Our Lord desires a deep, personal, and intimate relationship with you!

Sometimes this means opening your heart to the depths of your wretchedness, doubt, and fear and sharing it with Him. Then, listen to what He says. Do this repeatedly.

Additionally, you must find a wise, faithful, and experienced man you can confide in. He can help you reframe your situation in a way your wife cannot. Having at least one male friend of this type is essential to maintaining balance as a Christian man.

Above all, do not ignore these dark emotions. I have found in my own life that when a really negative event happens, the Lord will sometimes spare me from sexual temptations for a short while. Whether or not I have dealt with the emotions, the struggles return in due time. Do not ignore and bury these feelings. You will not be fit for the battle that will resume.

4. Avoid even the occasion of sin.

The "occasion of sin" may sound intimidating. All it means is a situation in which you would be tempted to commit a sinful action. Let me tell a cute story to highlight what I mean.

I live in a small town with a beautiful lake. All summer long, many tourists come to swim at the lake. It is common for young women to go to the beach wearing swimsuits that reveal far too much for my frail chastity to withstand.

One particular day, three men from the church were sitting on the sand and sharing about our lives. A few minutes into our conversation, several such women lay on their towels on the beach in front of where we were sitting. All three of us turned our bodies around so we were facing the arbor vitae trees that had previously been behind us. One of us declared, "Yes, brothers, the view is definitely better in this direction." We continued our conversation.

Those women were very attractive. There was no sin in the attraction, but we did enter the occasion of sin. If I had continued facing them, I would have fallen to temptation with additional looks. We stepped out of that occasion by turning around; the option to sin was removed.

Perhaps you are engaged. Do not be alone with your fiancée in a private space in the evening. This restriction is especially true if you both have had a few drinks. It is not sinful for two young people to spend time alone or to drink responsibly. We all know, however, what is likely to happen next if you do not take action to leave the occasion.

Similarly, perhaps you are married but know that you struggle with lustful thoughts toward other women. Make a commitment to your wife that you will not be alone with another woman in a compromising situation!

When I married, I had a job that sometimes required travel. I told my wife and my boss that I would neither travel alone with another woman nor go to dinner alone with a woman. My boss was not only OK with this but also agreed that it would avoid any potential accusations of misbehavior. I had no particular woman in mind, but avoiding a potentially dangerous situation was better!

Where are you falling? Look for patterns. Look within those patterns for what tends to happen before. Where are you? What are you doing? What other factors are involved? There are some situations, for example, that I will not drink alcohol because last time I fell. Be smart about this; seeing the bigger picture is usually easy.

YOU NEED FREEDOM

Men are stuck in a paradox. We have a deep, primal need to pursue freedom. We also must bind ourselves to a heavy burden and deep responsibility. Fulfillment only comes by pulling hard and making a difference in the world. Because of these two conflicting needs, there is a tension that we must all deal with. You will tend too much towards one at different points in your life.

When we are yoked to things of the world, we are less "free" to pursue the higher callings of our hearts. The greatest calling is to be free to pursue the love of the Lord. I wonder if this might be why there is no marriage in heaven—to make sure we are all as free as possible to love, praise, and worship God for all eternity.

Unfortunately, men often misuse and abuse their freedom. We often squander the capacity to love and praise God by excessively pursuing our interests and pleasures. Because of this propensity, many Christian authors emphasize the importance of being thoroughly yoked to our responsibilities. I am not going to disagree with them. To allow a sinful man (which we all are) unlimited freedom is to invite sin.

Many studies show that married men live longer and healthier lives than single men. As much as our wives sometimes can be difficult, the responsibilities they encourage us to carry help to keep us away from the sinful waste of freedom. Many men fear freedom, with good reason.

You still, however, need to express freedom in some capacity. You must have a pursuit, a hobby, or an activity that allows you to expand. Here are a couple of mine, why I choose them, and how I balance them:

- I go to the gym every morning. Working out allows me some time away from the kids and my wife. It is also essential for my physical and emotional health. I am less angry and tense when I exhaust my body than when I don't. There are some mornings when my family's needs are too great, and I don't get to go. I do not complain or hold a grudge (ideally, at least) when this happens.

- I love to hunt. Every fall, I try to plan one longer trip and a couple of shorter trips. These are times when I connect with God in a different and powerful way. I pray a great deal. The time away from the family rejuvenates me. I am free on these trips to do as I wish; sometimes, I take a middle day to rest the whole day. Some years, the trips don't happen or get canceled at the last minute. Regardless, I also try to make abundant time for my wife to take trips without children! We both need time without obligation.

- I plan frequent camping trips with some or usually all of the kids throughout the year. It's a time to break free of the daily grind and do something different.

- I occasionally do an impromptu beach trip with the kids so my wife has time alone.

- Sometimes, I jump on the quad to drive down a high-speed trail.

It doesn't matter what your expression of freedom looks like. It's about breaking free for a (well-chosen) moment to express this inner desire. I encourage you to include the Lord. Use this time to become a better person and to serve and love your family better.

If you deny this need for freedom, you will become pent-up, frustrated, and unable to submit yourself to the responsibilities you have fully. I do not encourage you to be reckless or inconsiderate. Plan your freedom well. Make sure all is in order, and be prepared for the reality that you may have to cancel your plans if something happens to your family. If you have many little children, you are in a phase where your events will be short. This restriction will pass.

YOU HAVE A "DARK" SIDE

Masculine energy and drive aren't always gentle or tame. We have this drive, on occasion, to tear down, to consume, to ravish. Many Christians believe these to be intrinsically disordered. Indeed, they often do lead to great damage and destruction when unregulated. Like all things created by God and given to mankind, they can be used for good or for evil.

Christ Himself gave exercise to his destructive drive on several occasions. The obvious example is when he cleared the temple of the money changers. Similarly, he regularly rebuked the Pharisees and other religious leaders. One might even propose that by allowing His passion, He chose for the destruction to go forward. Each of these, however, was ordered towards completing a greater and higher good.

One time, I stepped in front of a screaming man who appeared to be ready to hit a woman. A Christian man must protect his brother by preventing him from going too far. Had this screaming man continued his aggression, my strength might have been tested differently. It wouldn't be the first time.

We must embrace that our physical potential exists for a reason. God gave it to us to oppose the forces of evil in this world. We must not be afraid of them or view them as bad. To do so means we will not develop and understand what they can do.

One metaphor often used is that of wolves and sheepdogs. Strong sheepdogs are needed to guard the sheep from the wolves. The sheepdogs look very similar to the wolves in many ways, but not in their intent and self-control. Men must learn how to direct and control their strength correctly.

You see this challenge in preteens and especially teenage boys. I recently got into a healthy and fun wrestling match with my boys that utterly confused my daughters. "Why would they want to do such a thing?" my daughter questioned.

The boys need to understand their strength—how to use it with control and discretion. To do that, they require practice in a safe environment. My daughters had no desire to engage in such behavior at all!

You have a desire to engage in sex. You must do so in the proper ways and at the appropriate time. Priests, for example, are asked to sacrifice their desire for sex for a higher purpose. This sacrifice does not mean the desire is bad; they have learned to place that desire in its proper order. Perhaps you are married; you may then engage this desire appropriately with your wife—allow her to feel your passion and enthusiasm.

You have a desire for physical engagement and violence. Society may temper this into activities like watching sports. Still, it can come out destructively when we are scared, threatened, or intimidated. Engage this desire safely, similar to my boys when wrestling. Learn how your body responds—when do you go too far? When you understand and accept this dark side, it is much easier to submit it to the will of the Lord.

I love to play ultimate frisbee. On one terrible day, another man and I were having an unhealthy competition. It turned physical with some pushing and body checking. We went back and forth until I planted before him as he looked backward and delivered a potent hip check. He was knocked to the ground. When he got up, his fist was swinging at me.

I'm not proud of this day; I was out of line, for sure. However, when his fists started swinging, I knew enough of my dark side to know this was not the time to engage it. I'm happy to say that even though his third punch did land, I never attempted anything back. I was able to keep my cool and avoid the incident getting even bigger. A week later, he apologized, and we shook hands and could play together again.

Do not live in fear of your darker side. God has a plan even for that. Learn about it. Live into it. Gain strength so that you can choose when to turn up your danger level, as well as when not to.

There are moments with your wife (with her consent and also in the right place) to be more intense. There are moments of genuine danger when you become dangerous yourself. As with all else, give this to God and trust in Him.

ALLOW FEMININE BEAUTY TO POINT TO GOD

Feminine beauty is going to affect you. There is no point in trying to change this truth. You can either try to fight your biology or choose to channel this energy to do good. Ultimately, everything in this world is intended to draw us closer to God.

When you encounter feminine beauty, you will feel energized. If you wish, you can choose to allow this energy to spread into your entire body rather than merely your genitals. This energy can inspire you to give of yourself more deeply to those you love. It can free you from your bad mood or frustrations to be a happier, more caring version of yourself.

Consider feminine energy like a fine steak or a tasty drink (aged scotch is my choice). These experiences can provide a "reset" when we feel weighed down by the world and become discouraged. It is also possible to take them for granted, but when we allow this positive influence, it can radically change our moods.

Instead of merely using beautiful women as lustful objects for your fantasy, view them as a glimpse of the tiniest part of the beauty and wonder of God. Allow their beauty to inspire you to seek after God evermore. Draw the energy into your whole body and use it as fuel to give and serve others. You may be tempted to feel guilt or shame when this beauty energizes you. While you should never tolerate immoral actions, the energy you gain should not be wasted.

Your attraction to beauty is not the real purpose. As hard as it is to believe (and we all struggle with this), the beauty and goodness of God are greater than any of this world.

Allow yourself to see these attractions as merely a miniature of what is waiting for you in heaven. Consider it motivation to pick up your armor and sword to plunge back into the spiritual battle that is awaiting you. When you are wounded, perhaps an elvish maiden will show up not to satisfy your lust but to encourage you to keep fighting for God's will.

CONCLUSION

Everything that God makes is good, including you. You have sinned and fallen short of His glory, but do not fear. He offers mercy to help you stand again. The devil, by contrast, offers us many lies to distract us from the truths of God. Here are three common lies that many men struggle with:

- God's not really good; He doesn't really love me.
- I'm too broken; I've screwed up too much. God has given up on me.
- I have to hide my desires and behavior from God, or He will likely smite or reject me.

If you are gripped by one of these lies, seek help; the truth will set you free. Lean into the Bible and this book's truths and live your masculinity as God intends.

Be strong, powerful, bold, brave, daring, courageous, and humble! We have good reason to fear the lies of the devil, but he has even better reason to fear us! Be the soldier that God made you to be. You are on the winning team; Christ has already won the battle. He promises He will give you every grace and strength you need for this battle. Use them without hesitation or apology!

Be a strong, masculine man.

APPENDIX

LITANY OF HUMILITY

O Jesus! meek and humble of heart, hear me.

From the desire of being esteemed, *deliver me, Jesus.*
From the desire of being loved, deliver me, Jesus.
From the desire of being extolled, deliver me, Jesus.
From the desire of being honored, deliver me, Jesus.

From the desire of being praised, deliver me, Jesus.
From the desire of being preferred to others, deliver me, Jesus.
From the desire of being consulted, deliver me, Jesus.
From the desire of being approved, deliver me, Jesus.

From the fear of being humiliated, deliver me, Jesus.
From the fear of being despised, deliver me, Jesus.
From the fear of suffering rebukes, deliver me, Jesus.
From the fear of being calumniated, deliver me, Jesus.

From the fear of being forgotten, deliver me, Jesus.
From the fear of being ridiculed, deliver me, Jesus.
From the fear of being wronged, deliver me, Jesus.
From the fear of being suspected, deliver me, Jesus.

That others may be loved more than I,
Jesus, grant me the grace to desire it.

That others may be esteemed more than I,
Jesus, grant me the grace to desire it.

That, in the opinion of the world,
others may increase and I may decrease,
Jesus, grant me the grace to desire it.

That others may be chosen and I set aside,
Jesus, grant me the grace to desire it.

That others may be praised and I unnoticed,
Jesus, grant me the grace to desire it.

That others may be preferred to me in everything,
Jesus, grant me the grace to desire it.

That others may become holier than I,
provided that I may become as holy as I should,
Jesus, grant me the grace to desire it.

Amen.

ABOUT THE AUTHOR

Dr. Michael Jaquith is a Ph. D. Chemist who left the corporate world and now helps men everywhere discover how to get more of what they want and live the promise of abundant life.

By combining analytical science, psychology, and the time honored teachings of the Faith, Michael helps men who feel stuck, confused, and powerless to unlock those chains and find what they really want.

Michael is married with six children and lives in rural northern Idaho.

www.ingramcontent.com/pod-product-compliance
Lightning Source LLC
LaVergne TN
LVHW052028080426
835513LV00018B/2226